With an understanding of our limitations, we begin this odyssey, searching out and seeking to describe grace: Grace granted in weakness like Paul's—not merely in suffering and confusion, though there to be sure—but in our miserably weak perception of God's incessant and unrelenting gracious activity.

For in the middle of our variegated experiences, our triumphs and tragedies, our laughter and loneliness, torrents of God's grace explode all around us, bringing surprise, comfort, confrontation, costliness, nurture, and inspiration.

Also by John R. Wimmer
Published by Ballantine Books:

NO PAIN, NO GAIN

TORRENTS
OF
GRACE

John R. Wimmer

BALLANTINE BOOKS • NEW YORK

Scriptural quotations from the New English Bible are designated NEB. Otherwise, all quotations from scripture are the Revised Standard Version.

Library of Congress Catalog Card Number: 89-92439

ISBN 0-345-35971-2

Manufactured in the United States of America

First Edition: May 1990

To my Grandmother,
Mrs. Jessie L. Brown

CONTENTS

PREFACE

Martin Luther wrote, amid the sixteenth-century debates over the role of grace in the Christian faith, that his opponents seemed to possess "an abundance of leisure and plenty of paper on which to write falsities." The issue of grace, Luther complained, had given rise to a "*torrent of books*, questions, and opinions . . . for which the world has hardly room."[1]

If there was hardly room for the "torrent of books" about grace in the year 1520, one might justifiably wonder why another "torrent" now?

For one thing, Luther correctly complained of many common misunderstandings about grace. More recently, Leonardo Boff, a Brazilian Franciscan theologian, has observed that the centuries of technical discussions and theological manuals on grace have splendidly detailed our beliefs about grace. But there is a sense in which our talk *about* grace eludes the *experience* of grace. There is a dire need, says Boff, to ponder the experiential nature of God's grace:

There is a second way to approach the theme of grace. We can try to articulate the present-day experience of grace, expressing it in a way that is appropriate for our time, accessible, and acceptable to the community of faith. Here the emphasis is not on talking *about* grace but on letting grace do the talking (though all talk is *about* something). In other words, we want to create an idiom and a line of reflection which will make us conscious of the divine grace in which we now live, which will help us to detect the presence of God and his love in the world, quite apart from the fact that we may be thinking and talking about it.[2]

Torrents of Grace is written in this spirit of "letting grace do the talking," recognizing that it is still a book *about* the experience of grace. Each chapter will attempt to illuminate a different aspect of God's grace as we experience it in everyday life. I have intentionally omitted much of the classic, historical, and technical theological terms and debates on grace so that these experiences might speak more forcefully. I have too much admiration for the theological (and historical) enterprise to say these technical books and debates are of little importance, however. Quite the contrary—I spend a great deal of my time immersed in these profoundly significant issues! I am only suggesting there are indeed many excellent books of the technical/historical type and too few about everyday experiences of grace.

Another word should be said about this book's artificial thematic divisions of grace. From the beginning, please understand that grace is not divisible. We do not encounter differing graces, only different aspects of the same grace of God. As my friend Steve Harper has written in one of his books about John Wesley: "You do not have one kind of grace for one situation and another kind for some other situation. By the same token God does not give grace in bits and pieces. We define grace in different ways because of how we experience the grace on our end of the relationship. Grace comes to us at different stages in our spiritual pilgrimage, and it accomplishes different effects and evokes different responses. But it is all grace.''[3]

Above all, this book is about how the *experience* of God's grace can rebuild your life. Regardless of your current state of affairs, you can benefit from some spiritual reconstruction now and then. Whether you need only minor repairs or total remodeling, God's grace is constantly offering you the opportunity to grow spiritually. Like any home-improvement crusade, however, when you mend one part of the house you will probably begin to notice other areas in need of refurbishment. So it is when God's grace starts to rebuild your life. God is continually granting you the chance to rearrange your spirituality, to restructure it not on a faulty foundation of sand, but on the rock-solid base of grace. In this way, you, too, will be like the wise person who constructed a "house upon the rock, and the rain fell, and the floods came, and the winds blew and beat upon that house, but it did not fall, because it had been founded upon the rock" (Matt. 7:24–25). My hope is that you will allow your life to be rebuilt on the firm foundation of God's grace.

My life has been graced by a host of friends, family, and professionals who have helped mold this project into a community affair. As always, Jan Blaising is my favorite friend. Her constant love and support hold a special

place in my heart. I wish to thank my parents-in-law
Mark and Nona Blaising, Becky and Larry Axel, Michael
Snyder, and Pam Ramp Schneller for their careful read-
ings and helpful comments. My friend and colleague
Gary Forbes, along with the fine folks at Trinity United
Methodist Church in Lafayette, Indiana, have been true
sources of grace for me. I also want to express my grat-
itude to Martin Marty for his ever-gracious encouragement and for floating this manuscript into his already
overburdened "bathtub" reading list. I owe overdue
thanks to Juanita Denton for her aid during the writing
of my last book (and this one as well). Jan and Carl
Cowen helped me understand the wonders of Coventry
Cathedral; and gladly, this book completes my "barter
deal" with Don and Eva Paarlberg. My friend Toni Sim-
mons at Ballantine Books first encouraged me to write
on grace. Thanks also belong to Robert Wyatt who skill-
fully guided this project through its completion.

Finally, I can only begin to relate a lifetime of appre-
ciation for my grandmother, Jessie L. Brown, to whom
this book is lovingly dedicated.

CHAPTER I

Torrents of Grace—"Grace Every Day"

May God in the plentitude of his love
pour upon you the torrents of his grace,
bless you and keep you in his holy fear,
prepare you for a happy eternity,
and receive you at last into immortal glory.

—*Blessing at the consecration*
of the Coventry Cathedral

On the night of November 14, 1940, the town of Coventry, England, was the destination of a massive German air raid. To weaken British morale during the early days of war, Nazi air commanders had previously targeted London almost exclusively in their bombing missions. Since the luftwaffe's General Goering wanted to further demonstrate Germany's superior air power, he began a series of bombings on England's interior industrial and population centers beyond the capital.

Coventry was widely known not only as a significant munitions manufacturing city (therefore an important military target), it also somehow mystically symbolized much of British history and civility—with the fanciful legends of its eleventh-century founding by Leofric and Lady Godiva (complete with her famous horseback ride through town *au naturel*) and the three towering church spires that majestically dominated the quaint countryside.

Conventry has long been celebrated as the "City of the Three Spires."

According to Winston Churchill's Second World War memoirs, on that stark November evening nearly five hundred German aircraft unloaded six hundred tons of bombs and thousands of incendiary shells on Coventry. It was the most extensive air bombing yet witnessed in human history. The entire city center was demolished. Over a thousand people died and almost fifty-one thousand homes were damaged or destroyed. To "coventrate" entered the English language as a synonym for total destruction. Only the three great church spires, including the gothic tower of St. Michael's Cathedral, stood untouched amid the debris.

It was as if all that remained of the city's heart was the tall, isolated cross of Coventry Cathedral, casting a dreary shadow upon the hopes of thousands now made little more than rubble.

As the town and many lives were being rebuilt, plans were also made to reconstruct the cathedral. Work on the new church began in 1954. Symbolically, the old spire and ruins of St. Michael's were incorporated into the structure by the chief architect of the new cathedral, Basil Spence. The photograph on this book's cover is of the tower and the new cathedral "under construction." Two surviving relics of the bombing were fashioned into meaningful symbols of destruction and renewal. A few days after the air raid, two charred pieces of the oak roof beams salvaged from the ruins were tied together to form the now world-famous "Charred Cross." (Into the stone wall behind where this cross now stands, at the altar of the sanctuary ruins, are carved Christ's unforgettable words spoken from the cross: "Father Forgive.")

The second relic comes from the large fourteenth-century hand-forged nails used to secure the oak roof beams together. Hundreds of these nails littered the ruined sanctuary floor, fallen as the roof burned but surviving the intense heat. Fastened together, the nails also shape a cross, which has become the symbol of Coventry Cathedral's Ministry of International Reconciliation, an effort established to promote Christian reconciliation in a world divided by war and strife. Thousands of these crosses have been sent the world over to symbolize unity and reconciliation. In return, youth from all around the globe regularly come to Coventry to attend special seminars where they learn how to wage peace in international affairs.

On May 25, 1962, the beautifully modern Coventry Cathedral was at last consecrated, and St. Michael's old tower and ruins designated the Memorial Shrine of Reconciliation. The city that had been "coventrated" in war now formally dedicated its principal shrine to peace and understanding.

At the conclusion of the consecration day ceremony, an exceedingly simple but profound blessing was offered:

May God in the plentitude of his love
pour upon you the *torrents of his grace*,
bless you and keep you in his holy fear,
prepare you for a happy eternity,
and receive you at last into immortal glory.[1]

That second phrase, "the torrents of his grace," leapt off the page at me the first time I read it. It seemed like an entirely incongruous image, an oxymoron. A *torrent* is supposed to be turbulent, violent, chaotic—like a mountain stream swollen by a sudden downpour, a devouring forest fire, a sky raining explosives. At the same time, *grace* connotes something polite, forgiving to a fault, almost passively sweet—like urbane royalty, a demure ballerina, a delicately fragrant flower. What is a "torrent of grace"? I wondered.

I kept imagining that these words must have also sounded strange to those who had gathered at the Coventry consecration service. Wasn't it spiritually offensive, or at least in poor taste, to utter those words to the same people who not many years before had trembled at the torrent of *bombs* showering their lives with devastation? It was this very dissonance that attracted me to think and feel a bit more deeply about what the residents of Coventry were trying to say about the experience of grace through the words of their ritual.

When we look more closely at the Coventry story, we begin to understand how those who gathered to consecrate their new cathedral had been ravaged by grace. Certainly this was not the same polite grace we associate with stoic courtly manners or the sweet grace of a beautiful object. It was *God's grace*, poured out in torrents from a plentitude of love, made visible in a tempestuous world by a symbol that invites renewal from destruction, reconciliation from conflict, peace from war—the symbol of the cross. In the midst of destruction's pain, grace came to rebuild. But it was not merely a restructuring of steel, brick and mortar, stained glass; grace came to create a wholly and holy new structure promoting reconciliation and peace. When people band together and rebuild their shattered lives with faith—this is truly a gracious act of God.

Therefore, the Coventry story is above all a model through which we can see how God's grace rebuilds lives. For these persons, infused with divine grace, have constructed a monument transcending the painful effects of time, circumstance, and place, to reach toward the paradoxical truth of God's love so well described in their eloquent dedicatory blessing.

From a plentitude of love, by God's grace—*torrents of grace*—Coventry saw devastation redeemed! Likewise, your life can be rebuilt by grace!

Describing Grace

Before we can speak more specifically about how grace can restructure your spiritual life, we must talk about what grace is. While defining God's grace is beyond the boundaries of human expression, describing how grace affects our lives is not. In fact, the task of trying to define and describe grace has preoccupied theologians, church councils, countless laity, and pastors for nearly two millennia. Yet the story of Coventry Cathedral demonstrates that grace is something we can experience and describe, even if after centuries of discussion and debate we still may not comprehend the fullness of God's grace. For divine grace is the unexpected power from beyond ourselves that comes to us and springs within us, enabling us to live the gift of life and die the gift of death with more meaning, faith, hope, and love. With the benefit of witnesses from many centuries, and through our own experiences with grace, we understand that sometimes grace comes as comfort. Other times it painfully prods us. It is free, but costs much. Always grace comes to help us if we will perceive and receive it. It is the gift of God's own love interjected into our lives regardless of how good or bad we've been. Grace is how God encounters our ordinariness, touching life with a nourishing, loving Presence.

Torrents of grace in our own lives may seem difficult to detect chiefly because most of us look not for torrents, but trickles of grace. Since grace is both elusive and unforeseen, many of us frequently fail to recognize its appearance amid the mundane. While it is one thing to grasp grace's role in rebuilding monumental cathedrals ripped apart in world war, it is quite another to discover grace subtly flowing through our normal workaday numbness or in the dim drudgery of necessary chores.

Regardless of your particular circumstances, be they exciting, excruciating, or humdrum, grace is always present in your life. But even though it is ever-present, grace is not always apparent. Like the triumvirate of faith, hope, and love, grace seems to fade in and out of our consciousness, somewhat dependent upon the ups and downs of our current experiences. Yet because it is God's unexpected gift, we are seldom well served by trying to *find* grace. In truth, we must retrain ourselves to be *found* by grace, by God. Being found by grace comes not from our own excellent efforts to be good or faithful or loving or hopeful or even graceful. Grace's "foundness" comes from an openness to God's extraordinary unexpectedness. When we try to acquire or possess or grab God's grace, we chase after hollow facsimilies that do not satisfy us; but when we permit ourselves to be found by grace's surprises, to be alert for its strange but meaningful contours surfacing daily, we may unintentionally find ourselves experiencing more penetrating dimensions of God's wholeness and love.

As we will discuss more fully later, allowing grace to find you is how your spiritual life begins to be restruc-

tured. Yet from the start, you shouldn't assume grace
will always make you happy. God's grace indeed sometimes comforts you; but it may also *confront* you in ways
you do not expect.

The Apostle Paul came to understand in a special way
this distinction about grace when he confessed to the
Corinthian church his so-called "thorn in the flesh."
Apparently several believers in Corinth had been wary
about Paul's leadership and suspicious of his authenticity
as an official "apostle" (since he was not one of the
original twelve with Jesus). Throughout the Corinthian
correspondence, Paul tried to bolster his credibility by
attesting to his particular apostolic authority, appealing
to evidence of persecution and hardships, as well as by
presenting unique revelations given him by the Lord.
While he admits that highlighting his resumé may resem-
ble mere "boasting," unlike an unabashed braggart, Paul
continues by honestly exposing his profoundest weakness:

> And to keep me from being too elated by the abun-
> dance of revelations, a thorn was given me in the
> flesh, a messenger of Satan, to harass me, to keep
> me from being too elated. Three times I besought
> the Lord about this, that it should leave me; but he
> said to me, "My grace is sufficient for you, for my
> power is made perfect in weakness.
>
> 2 Corinthians 12:7–9a

For centuries interpreters have tried to ascertain Paul's
"thorn" (or literally "stake") in the flesh. Some scholars
conjecture it was an onerous physical ailment such as
epileptic seizures or chronic migraine headaches. Others

assert the thorn was of a spiritual nature, perhaps sexual temptation or vicious persecution from those opposed to his message. While it is interesting to speculate about things of which we can never be certain, all these possibilities are not as important as the fact that to Paul his thorn was excruciatingly *real*. What is most significant is that in his exasperation, including three desperate petitions to God for healing or relief from his distress, Paul writes the Lord said to him very simply, "My *grace* is sufficient for you, for my power is made perfect in weakness" (emphasis added).

Again we may feel stymied by this image's jarring incongruity, or at least its apparent irrelevance: In a world of geopolitical military maneuverings, brutal hostage-taking, cloak-and-dagger secret arms deals, multibillion-dollar corporate mergers with their inside-trading scandals, doesn't Paul understand that power and weakness are opposites? You don't gain influence in this rough-and-tumble world by being a wimp! If God wants to give you *power*, a healthy investment portfolio and some sympathetic friends in high places would be much more effective in crushing those who dare to challenge righteousness. The meek may inherit the earth, but they don't enlarge their market share.

Paul's portrayal of God's intention is quite different. When we are charmed open by Paul's candor, we, too, come out from underneath the blanket of our own bravado enough to perceive he is describing an encounter with God that grants a kind of power very different than military, financial, or political power. And once more, like the Coventry blessing, a confounding truth about God's encounter with us comes to the fore. As with Paul, in moments of weakness—those times when we reach the limits of our own powers and can no longer foster the illusion we are captain of our own soul—we, too, learn that God's grace has its best chance of sinking in. When our carefully constructed defenses and façades that mask us from God are dismantled, often involuntarily, at least expected times and in unforeseen circumstances, grace interjects God's sufficiency to meet our need, to challenge our stubbornness, or to *empower* our lives.

With braggadocio quickened not by pride but by graceful humility, Paul boasts more wildly after his confession and experience of grace:

> I will all the more gladly boast of my weaknesses, that the power of Christ may rest upon me. For the sake of Christ, then, I am content with weaknesses, insults, hardships, persecutions, and calamities; for when I am weak, then I am strong.
>
> 2 Corinthians 12:9b–10

While Paul's words comfort and inspire those who suffer thorny problems of the flesh, they correspondingly challenge the relatively narrow perceptions of grace held by us all. And why shouldn't our understanding of grace be incomplete? How can we fathom with the relatively puny boundaries of our hearts and minds the extent of God's infinite grace and love? How can we capture and isolate and microscopically analyze a reality as pervasive (and as elusive) as grace? As we have seen, defining grace is beyond our capacities. But describing grace is not; it is something we must try to do that we may be ready and able to receive it.

A Look Ahead

With such an understanding of our limitations we begin this odyssey, searching out and seeking to describe grace—grace granted in weakness like Paul's—not merely in suffering and confusion, though there to be sure—but also in our miserably weak perception of God's incessant and unrelenting gracious activity. Perhaps, utilizing clues from the biblical message, guided by the symbolic example of the Coventry blessing, and instructed by masters of the past who have wrestled with these same questions and limits, we, too, may rediscover a sense of grace rebuilding our spiritual lives. For in the middle of our variegated experiences, our triumphs and tragedies, our laughter and loneliness, torrents of God's grace explode all around us—bringing surprise, comfort, confrontation, costliness, nurture, and inspiration.

These elements of grace are the topics of the chapters to follow. Let's briefly look ahead and introduce these themes that will form the remainder of this book:

As we will continue exploring Paul's honest confessions and insights, especially in his conversion experience, we will see it is grace's unexpected nature that inclines us to see only trickles of grace (chapter 2). Americans especially exacerbate this tendency because we are accustomed to expect as a birthright an abundance of that which many others accept as unmerited grace. While plentitude surrounds and undergirds our entire cultural life-style, it is no secret we have become a ''throwaway'' society, thoughtlessly squandering astonishing amounts of resources, both human and material. Like an obese child fattened on junk food but suffering malnutrition, we spiritually starve while a bountiful banquet of grace is spread before us. At the same time increasing numbers of people suffer loneliness, many churches and community organizations offering vital human contact are shrinking; we are tortured by guilt for our faultless deeds while effectively ignoring true guilt for huge crimes we condone by omission or sheer resignation; we longingly search out helpful spiritual guidance for our peripatetic lives at the same time we schedule our days so full that even our spiritual exercises must be squeezed into the busy executive's calendar. We are afflicted with creating and ordering our abundance, so full of it we cannot perceive or receive grace's surprises.

What is shameful about this predicament is not how we have wronged God as much as how we have missed God's wondrously comforting grace (chapter 3). Quite aside from the undue stress we cause by overextending ourselves to the exclusion of surprise, even a normal life's pilgrimage may be described as a "maze." While aristocrats and royalty once constructed intricate labyrinths out of well-manicured garden hedges to confuse and amuse themselves and their guests, life's maze for most of us is not very laughable. We sometimes feel like wayward rodents locked in a twisted rat race. The ubiquitous presence of grief, hurt, hunger, poverty, discrimination, and many more tragic elements all seem to take the fun out of the playful maze. At times it even seems like God has crafted a cruel joke, leading the blind and gullible down dead-end paths, insisting we believe that integrity, honesty, morality, and kindness are their own reward while most of the evidence we see around us would indicate the contrary.

Yet even in the knotty, morally confounding, mazelike realm that seems to surround us, grace comes as *comfort*.

As Paul has reminded us, it is in these moments of weakness, these experiences of our limits, that grace interjects itself most noticeably. And what grace offers in confusing circumstances comes in many more ways than mere soothing assurance. Comfort includes forgiveness, hope, encouragement, fellowship, friendship, and much more.

Moments of vulnerability not only present optimal opportunities for grace's comfort, they are often our most challenging times. They are moments not of comfort but of *confrontation* (chapter 4). There is a rather whimsical saying among the clergy that their job is "to comfort the afflicted and afflict the comfortable." (Actually, ministers borrowed the phrase from Joseph Pulitzer, who coined it to describe the task of a journalist.) The degree to which this statement is true is to the degree it is analogous with grace. While in life's mazes God's grace certainly comforts, it can also *dis*-comfort those who grow too self-satisfied or complacent in their spiritual/moral lives. Jesus' militant proclamation was no dull platitude: "I come not to bring peace but a sword!" (Matt. 10:34). God's grace accuses and recriminates our improper priorities and values, our trifling faith and behavior. Grace may bring strife, not peace, to our hearts. Although this comes as anything but comfort, it is important to recognize this dis-ease as a gift of grace nonetheless. Only in our willingness to struggle with this darkness may we see it is not darkness at all, only another form of God's grace trying to enlighten blighted aspects of our sinful, limited spiritual selves. This same confrontive grace not only makes demands on us as individuals; God's judgment challenges our overlapping national, denominational, and international narrowness.

In this light, to sing "America, America, God shed His grace on thee," takes on a much different meaning.

God's confrontive grace therefore sheds light on the "cost of our discipleship" as much as it offers forgiveness for our sins. As grace confronts our invalid assumptions and warped ethical intentions and actions, one of the most important values it informs is the "cost of grace" (chapter 5). Balancing this free and costly nature of grace is a very delicate matter. For on the one hand, we must affirm the free nature of grace—Christ's free offering of himself for all humanity, revealing the unlimited (and unmerited) riches of God's love. On the other hand, free grace is no license for immorality. Nothing is quite so sickening as grace used as an excuse to justify one's self-serving behavior. Grace *costs*. (It cost Jesus his life!) If grace is reduced to "forgiving" while "forgetting" the cost, it has been irreparably cheapened, as Dietrich Bonhoeffer so profoundly declared. But if grace is so costly, how can it be free? How much does grace cost?

Like so many questions of faith, our probing is informed by Christ: The cost of grace is as free and as costly as one dying on a cross. For such a tragic symbol attaches a cost to grace we cannot afford to purchase in any way; yet it also demonstrates how freely grace is given to all who are touched by the depth of God's self-sacrifice. In the cross was demonstrated the difficult balancing act: Free and costly grace harnessed together demand a free and costly response.

From the multifaceted example of Christ, we see grace is a most sacred gift. Christ is the symbol and reality of the grace granted by God in every moment of every day, dispensed in many mysterious ways, each of which should be received sacramentally. For life itself is a sac-

rament of grace (ch. 6). Through the church, the sacraments, God's creation, family, relationships, study,
God bestows grace upon all who will "listen to their
lives" and alert themselves to God's graceful beckoning.

Torrents of grace explode all around those who are not
deafened to its everydayness. For it is in the everyday
sights, sounds, smells, and touches of life that God's
grace may be sensed. That is, *if* we are open to God's
surprises.

CHAPTER II

Surprising Grace— "Grace Unexpected"

We cannot transform our lives, unless we allow them to be transformed by that stroke of grace. It happens; or it does not happen. And certainly it does not happen if we try to force it upon ourselves, just as it shall not happen so long as we think, in our self-complacency, that we have no need of it.[1]

—Paul Tillich

To speak of grace is to say that the things most worth experiencing are the things that are unexpected. Our explicit anticipations will be fulfilled or disappointed. But those things we do not anticipate, those things that come as surprise—ah, those are the moments that reshape us and nurture us for yet more surprises.[2]

—Robert McAfee Brown

*O*n a crisp autumn Saturday afternoon my wife Jan and I set out for two estate auctions to see if any collectable antiques were for sale. We enjoy auctions; not only are they excellent opportunities to pick up bargains, they are also a permissible way to "snoop" into the private lives of all sorts of interesting people. You can tell a lot about people by what they own, use, save, and discard.

The two auctions we found that day were in different settings. One was conducted in a modest frame home in a sleepy little town, the other at a huge isolated farmhouse out in the flat prairie land some miles from our city. I was surprised to see identical items for sale at both locations.

As we were rummaging through the ordinary collection of household appliances, glassware, and kitsch at the small house, I happened to glance at a compact, thick-walled iron chest—a "safe" for storing valuables. This safe from the 1930s had obviously been used extensively, evidenced by a shiny ring around the combination spindle where the paint had been worn off. I didn't think much about this curiosity until we arrived at the sprawling country auction later that afternoon. There, as I was once again sorting through tools, vegetable canning jars, and old books, I saw nestled in the junk an item that looked familiar—it was another well-worn safe! It was even the same name brand and size as the other.

The curious coincidence of two safes in one day made me wonder why these two older folks, both living in rural isolation, should have been so cautious. Then it occurred to me that they had lived through the Great Depression. Those were the days before the Federal Deposit Insurance Corporation (FDIC) insured bank deposits, a program begun in the New Deal to bolster a sense of confidence in our nation's troubled banking system. There was good reason to inaugurate such security, since hundreds of banks in the Depression era were forced to close when they could not satisfy fearful depositors' demands for their savings. (With the recent Savings and Loan crisis we can appreciate once again this need for assurance.) For many people the "scare" became a reality when they lost their life savings, homes, farms, jobs, and businesses in the financial panic. I am not old enough to remember the tough times that followed, though I have heard stories from members of my family and read enough history to know it was an extremely difficult period.

Considered in such an atmosphere of uncertainty, it

became easier to understand why two different homes, far removed from any city's crime and vandalism, would contain a safe. A "safe" is just what the name implies; a safety, security, a confidence insulating one's treasures from theft and harm. The human inclination to try and keep one's self, family, and possessions "safe" is perfectly natural—especially when one has suffered from a *real* threat and loss as during the Depression.

So the idea of a "safe" also has a *symbolic* meaning. "Being safe" represents not only our attempts to avert economic hardship, it is also a metaphor for a spiritual urge. We seek our own spiritual safety under various guises. In order to avoid confronting spiritual inadequacies from which we would rather steer clear, we insulate ourselves within many thick walls—walls of holier-than-thou piety, walls of cynicism or skepticism, "safe" walls of abundance and possessions.

From Safe to Credit Card

These impressions represent a transformation that has taken place in the societal foment of recent decades. I am not one to look back on the halcyon "good old days," for I believe they never really existed. Of course, there *were* good times in the past. But in general people, events, governments, and beliefs were just as cruel and corrupt in the past as they may be now, perhaps even more so. We must resist the temptation to romanticize the past. Many changes have been for the better, others for the worse. Either way, in our magnificent and terrible century, certain developments have shaped our nation into what historian Warren Susman has called "a culture of abundance." As Susman and a host of other cultural critics have observed, our society has been transformed from one emphasizing the value of producing and saving resources to one valuing accumulation and spending.[3]

As the presence of the auction safes indicate, the immediate cause of yesteryear's penchant for accumulation and saving came from the scarcity of the Depression era and the rationing of essential goods during World War II. Because money and material were both sparse during those lean years, resources were to be frugally preserved and recycled. We either remember those times vividly or have relatives and acquaintances who do. Theologian Joseph Sittler told of his aunt who displayed that era's attitude when she saved all sizes of boxes in which to store the massive amounts of knickknacks she collected. These boxes and their contents were organized, labeled, and grouped with meticulous precision. Sittler reported that one of the funniest things he ever saw was one of her tiny boxes labeled "pieces of string too short to save"![4] I'll wager that you know someone like Sittler's aunt!

"Those were the days" when nothing was discarded. Double-digit unemployment, long soup kitchen lines, sugar and gasoline rationing coupons were all daily reminders of scarcity. More importantly, this urge to save and accumulate became a *mentalité*, an unconscious inner compulsion to provide goods and comfort for loved ones even in lean years. During the war especially it became a *community* obligation to be frugal. One motto prevailed: We must all work together and save for tomorrow, for no one knows what hardships a new day will bring.

Moreover, another basic human emotion exacerbates this impulse. It is every parent's dream to make life better for their children, no matter what the circumstances.

Therefore, during Depression and war years, countless parents enduring hardship made the silent vow: My children are not going to have to suffer this! Hard work, saving, and accumulating have largely fulfilled this parental promise. Indeed, most of their children did not have to endure the same kind of poverty.

But these economic conditions have ironically created an unanticipated spiritual problem. For conflicting with this older view is a more recent mind-set in America, born in an economic climate of plenty, not paucity. Our "culture of abundance" has maintained the inner compulsion to accumulate but has discarded (or has never been forced to learn) its beneficial motivations. Our parents have taught us well the value of accumulating possessions—but many of us have not experienced the scarcity that makes such saving necessary! People who have known no shortage of string no longer remember why they must save, they just vaguely sense they are supposed to accumulate. Gone is the motivation to provide for a possible future shortage ("saving for a rainy day") or to sacrifice for the larger good of the community. Now that our nation enjoys tremendous abundance we still somehow feel that we must garner always more. When this accumulative urge is compounded and projected on a larger scale, the amount of resources involved becomes immense.

In sharp contrast with our ancestors, the amount of goods we "require" has become so huge that by necessity we have become a "throwaway" society. Today's "needs" are yesterday's "wants." The average American, for example, only saved 3 percent of after-taxes income, compared to a rate six or seven times greater saved by Japanese workers. Gertrude Stein, quoted by

Ernest Hemingway at the beginning of his novel, *The Sun Also Rises*, told young Americans of the 1920s they were "a lost generation." We, on the other hand, are a *grabby* generation. Rather than save pieces of string too short to save, we throw away pieces too long to use!

Possessions thereby lose their importance because we are compelled to accumulate and possess ever more. Hence we create an upwardly spiraling cycle of expectations. We work, buy, accumulate, spend, and dream of having more. This is the American Dream—to soar always higher, dig always deeper, aspire always bigger. We are scheduled to climb the ladder of success, which will move us from a two-bedroom apartment to a three-bedroom house, and finally to a lavish estate on Country Club Lane. Advancement moves us from a Chevy to an Oldsmobile or Buick, on the way to a Cadillac or Mercedes. (I am somewhere between the Chevy and Oldsmobile stage!) These ever-upward spiraling expectations are applied to virtually every aspect of our lives.

Yet because our reach exceeds our grasp (or our spending surpasses our earnings and savings), what we accumulate in the end is not only material but *debt*. Often—as with our gargantuan national deficit—our debts, both personal and collective, become so burdensome we cannot help feeling they can never be repaid. Much of our affluence is built on a faulty foundation of overextended credit.

The symbolic metaphor in our own time has shifted from an iron-walled safe to a fragile house of cards—*credit* cards, that is!

Let me say that I believe that the American Dream is in many ways an excellent motivator. We should continue to strive for progress in many fields such as health care and food production. Borrowing is essential for these advances as well as making possible a variety of modern services and products that make life more meaningful and enjoyable. Economists tell us that the element of incentive is of prime importance to a healthy, growing economy. "Productivity" and "competitiveness" are the catchwords of success. And motivations to succeed keep most of us very busy, if not earning a higher standard of living, then working for better schools for our children, more efficient community agencies, or effective ministries through our churches. The sheer personal and institutional energy required to maintain that which we already possess will combine with attempts to create even more abundance to keep us working for some time to come. We are, and will continue to be, extremely busy simply keeping our abundance in order.

Paying Your Dues

Despite its benefits, this societal urge to earn—in part what sociologists have called the "work ethic"—creates a severe dilemma for our understanding of the gift of grace. If indeed much of our cultural affluence is built on a faulty foundation of overextended credit, so, too, is much of our spirituality built on shaky foundations that misinterpret grace. For the notion of *earning* God's favor is contrary to the experience of free grace, no matter if you are wealthy and successful or impoverished and struggling. On the one hand, the dream of soaring higher for many people spirals not ever-upward but downward and out of control, ending with a tragic crash. If we attempt to explain God's favor in terms of material possessions, where is God's grace for the person whose business has failed, or the one who did not receive the promotion at work, or the one left unemployed because a corporate merger forced the company to cut even long-time faithful workers from the payroll? Unfortunately, people who experience economic difficulties often falsely feel as if they do not *deserve* God's grace.

On the other hand, the gap between those who have managed to succeed and the unsuccessful feeds an erroneous assumption that unlimited opportunity exists for everyone. Unlike the "have-nots" who feel as though they do not deserve grace, the "haves" often falsely feel as if they have merited an extra measure of divine favor as a reward for their hard work. This type of viewpoint produces, as we will see, a kind of spiritual numbness that is far removed from the experience of God's free, unmerited grace.

Both of these attempts to make grace into an earned commodity stem from a quite elemental human instinct. In his book, *Guilt and Grace*, psychologist Paul Tournier has written that embedded deep within the human psyche is the need to affirm that "everything must be paid for."[5] Subconsciously we feel nothing is "free." In fact, few things *are* free. Therefore, when something happens to us, either good or bad, we feel a sense of responsibility or guilt. If something good occurs, we somehow feel guilt because we did not really deserve or earn it—our good fortune was not paid for. On the other hand, if something bad happens, we somehow feel responsible because we imagine we have done something wrong and have received nothing but what we deserved. Success or failure, good luck or bad, we cannot escape this sense of guilt when we expect everything to carry a price tag. The power of such responsibility, says Tournier, is so intense and seemingly insoluble that it robs many persons—even very spiritual persons—from appropriating grace.

Many of our common cultural maxims bespeak this fixation. In the workplace you are constantly reminded you must "pay your dues" if you are to succeed, just as the Economics 101 professor propounds Milton Friedman's dictum, "There is no such thing as a free lunch." These ideas are so deeply held that we are seldom aware of their influence. For example, a friend of mine had diligently filled out a fast-food restaurant card that entitled her to a free salad-bar lunch after purchasing twelve meals. One noontime after she had fulfilled the requirements, she went to enjoy her free lunch. She stepped up to the counter and ordered the salad and a glass of water as she chatted with a few friends. Without thinking, she reached into her purse and handed the cashier a ten-dollar bill to pay for her salad. The cashier gave her an odd expression and handed back the money, saying, "Your lunch is *free* . . ." My friend was so taken aback it took her a few seconds to realize it didn't need to be paid for!

This episode does not refute the infamous "free lunch" economics lesson—clearly the "free" salad came only after purchasing twelve salads. But it does indicate that when something which need not be paid for comes our way, we often have difficulty perceiving and receiving it. It is little wonder the reality that "everything must be paid for" is a fact of life with which we must become accustomed if we are to survive.

Overlapping this psychic and economic reality is the spiritual version of "paying your dues." Sociologist Max Weber's classic book, *The Protestant Ethic and the Spirit of Capitalism*, tells how economic and religious motives are connected and how this particular urge to earn has worked itself out in European and American history.[6] The book tells the sociological story of how modern capitalism and the "work ethic" were given birth by sixteenth- and seventeenth-century Protestantism. Weber believed that the Protestant idea of the "priesthood of all believers" enabled people of all vocations or "callings" to view their occupational work as a way to respond to God's grace (the word *vocation* comes from the Latin *vocatio*, which means "to call"). Previously the only way to be a Christian in one's "vocation" was to be "called" by God to be a priest, monk, or nun—to be a "religious" rather than a "secular," as they say in the Roman Catholic tradition. Weber noticed Protestantism taught that one's response to God required diligence and "industry" in work, frugality in spending, and faithfulness in stewardship and giving. Conversely, idleness, "sloth," and poverty were considered signs of moral weakness and therefore sinful. Who has not heard at one time or another, "Idle hands are the devil's workshop"?

Furthermore, because of an unshakable belief in the "predestination" of some souls to salvation and others to damnation, one's diligence and success at work became an indication of whether or not one was counted among God's "elect," those who were preordained to salvation. One's "productivity" became a major criterion for determining if God's grace had touched one's life. Success signified grace. If one was poor and slothful, grace must be absent. Anxiety over one's eternal destiny thereby impelled one to work hard and save to *prove* one was saved by grace. Savings proved you were saved! Such "industry" and frugality naturally led to accumulation of capital, which stimulated large-scale private

business enterprise not possible under medieval feudal-
ism or mercantile economic systems.

Busyness begat business! Our strong Puritan heritage
inoculated us with a huge dose of what Weber called
"worldly asceticism." Benjamin Franklin's secularized
Puritan aphorisms are second nature to our culture and
illustrate the point: "A penny saved is a penny earned,"
"Early to bed and early to rise, makes a man healthy,
wealthy, and wise," and "God helps them that help
themselves."

This "Weber thesis" (the validity of which has been
debated in mountains of books) aptly demonstrates in
history and society how some people habitually feel that
they must pay their dues to earn salvation or to be accepted by God. Likewise, in our modern life's cluster of
spiritual, economic, psychological, and social concerns,
we feel we must keep proving ourselves worthy of God's
acceptance.

David Seamands, in his book, *Healing Grace*, calls
this "the performance trap." Because our culture teaches
us that to "make it" means to "perform" on the job,
we feel we must prove our *worth* by what we have *earned*.
Unfortunately, many churches reinforce this theological
fallacy by making one's earning power an unspoken requisite for admission—one must work for the "proper"
company, be "dressed for success," and belong to the
"correct" race or socioeconomic class. Though the mar-
quee in front of the affluent church says "Everyone Welcome," most poor folks know the invitation is not for
them even if they can't read. That is how effectively even
religious people communicate their belief that grace must
be earned.

Worth and Grace

Although Tournier spoke of the sense of guilt arising out of the need to "pay our dues," this urge is rooted in our sense of *worth*. We feel we must *work*, earn, and succeed to be *worth*-y. The outward manifestation of spending and accumulation only masks a deeper inward dissatisfaction. While some feel guilty for wrongdoing and attempt to correct the wrong by excessive "right-doing" (as Tournier shows), others who feel unworthy try to overcompensate by creating a frantic and frenetic life-style, attempting to *earn* acceptance through material accumulation and busyness (as Weber shows). But neither life-style soothes an uneasy conscience: we are never really quite sure *whose* acceptance we are trying to earn or if we have secured it. The "debt" mentality drives despair even deeper. A "debt" must be paid for; but if it is too large, we feel evermore indebted and anxious and unable to repay.

There is a special irony in this misunderstanding about grace, for the Protestant Reformation began as a reaction *against* the association of God's grace with the requirement of earning it by "good works." God's grace and acceptance, the reformers taught, is in no way contingent upon your ability to earn it or pay for it. That God's unmerited grace and acceptance should become associated with wealth and worth is a supreme betrayal of the true meaning of grace. As we will see when we discuss the "cost" of grace (chapter 5), we must not confuse God's free and gracious initiative toward us with our costly response to God's grace.

But churches sometimes fall into the trap nevertheless. To attract people who feel unworthy and who are in a frenzy to succeed, some churches offer a gospel of success aimed at making self-acceptance palpable at the expense of free grace. According to this false gospel, Jesus is at once a supreme psychotherapist and a bubbly community leader, one whose sole mission is to help us feel good about ourselves. (Bruce Barton's bestselling book of the 1920s, *The Man Nobody Knows*, and a host of similar books since, would make us believe Jesus was really a slick salesman sent to teach us the secrets of success—hardly the same man whose life ended in what the world would consider utter *failure* by death on a cross!) Churches subscribing to this misinterpretation of a back-slapping Jesus offer worship services that contain nothing but uplifting inspiration, have only "nice" sermons preached by tamed pastors, and feature angelic children singing fluffy songs about "gentle Jesus, meek and mild" frolicking among his docile little lambs.

Beware of churches that dress Jesus in sheeps' clothing. These churches incongruently promote aerobics classes to exercise obese congregants into "firm believers," ice-cream socials to raise money for the hungry, and tropical island mission trips on which the "missionaries" take more suntan lotion for themselves than medicine for the poor. The programs of such churches produce plastic pastors and indulgent lay people who try not to shape the world, but to ape the world's success. Their chief goal becomes virtually indistinguishable from that of any cutthroat business—to increase the market share, to grow at any cost. And growth at any cost means developing a slick public relations campaign offering a saccharine self-acceptance that undercuts true grace with a very cheap price. Senator Mark Hatfield has given a name to this kind of congregation: "The Church of the Warm Jacuzzi."

While abundance makes some people look to the church to baptize their greed with splashy sanctimony, the abundance of others creates a false sense of independence and security. A minister friend of mine visited a family in his church who harbored this attitude. Several years before, he had paid a visit at their request during a crisis—the father had lost his job and they were faced with an uncertain financial future. With new employment everything changed. Now my friend noticed all the trappings of success in their beautiful home and a radically changed posture toward faith. This time the family was uneasy during his pastoral visit. Abruptly, the woman stood up in midconversation, signaling to my friend that it was time for him to leave. Ushering him hastily out the door, she mentioned politely, "Everything is going so well we really don't need God right now. We'll let you know if we do . . ." It was as if God were some sort of good luck charm, a rabbit's foot to rub in distress or discard in plenty. They were now "safe" within the walls of abundance and indifference. Such an attitude reveals a scurrilously weak understanding of God's grace.

Our spiritual problems and needs are much more complex than seeking a God and churches to help us feel good about ourselves through psychological, physical, and spiritual gymnastics. For the root of the dilemma is this: We are so encompassed by images of worth that are tied to accumulation and abundance—to "paying our dues"—we can no longer be *surprised* by anything free. Because grace by its nature is free, it is surprising. When we stop looking for anything free, we lack the capability of being surprised. We falsely feel we must be graced

the "old-fashioned way"—we must *earn* it. The difficulty with this idea is what Jesus was talking about when
he said it was easier for a camel to go through the eye
of a needle than for a rich person to enter God's Kingdom
(Matt. 19:24). Encased in safes with thick walls to store
our treasures and our debts, it is difficult for anything
unexpected to enter. And so we fumble to find the right
combination of life, happiness, wholeness, and worth that
will unlock our seemingly "safe" prisons. We have ac-
cumulated and spent and indebted ourselves to the limits,
but more does not satisfy. There is little room left in the
spiritual safe for any surprises. There is little room for
grace.

About-Face Grace

The scriptures tell us that if we are to allow grace to
enter our lives as surprise, something wholly unanticipated, we must above all learn to expect the unexpected
from God. We must reconsider our deeply held attitudes
about "paying our dues." For God is offering more grace
in our lives than we are willing to receive. We must,
then, alert ourselves to God's unexpected way of turning
things upside-down. For if God is to pierce through our
thick-walled safe, it will likely be in a quite unanticipated
way.

No biblical story tells of *surprising grace* better than
that of Paul's conversion. For centuries it has been told
and retold as the model conversion experience. Yet some
of its meaning has been obscured by exaggeration of
Paul's later apostolic glory at the expense of his unsavory
life prior to the Damascus Road incident. Paul's personal
journey is much more like ours than we may think. For

a long time he was blind to surprise—until (paradoxically) he was blinded into seeing what Paul Tillich called
"that unexpected stroke of grace."

If we were to choose a contemporary occupation to
describe him before conversion, we could very well say
Paul was a "terrorist." A terrorist is, of course, a person
from a particular political and religious persuasion who
attempts to force influence through acts of terror and
violence. The results can be devastating and explosive,
as the steady stream of bad news from the Middle East
and elsewhere reminds us.

Paul was no less zealous in his ruthlessness than modern terrorists. Moreover, he was famous for his brutal
tactics. The apostle wrote to the church in Galatia, "For
you have heard of my former life . . . how I persecuted
the church of God violently and tried to destroy it . . . so
extremely zealous was I for the traditions of my fathers"
(Gal. 1:13–14). Paul held the cloaks of those who stoned
Stephen (Acts 7:54–60). Acts even reports, "And Saul
was consenting in his death" (8:1). By modern legal
standards this would make him an accomplice to murder.

It may seem extreme to suggest Paul was a terrorist.
A mafia-type "hit man" isn't exactly the ideal mental
picture we entertain about *Saint* Paul. I still remember
the painting of Paul reproduced in the Bible my parents
gave me as a child. He was portrayed dictating a letter
to his scribe, cowled in a brown alb that made him look
like an ultrareligious monk. The light encircling his head
glowed like a halo. His posture was depicted in a strik-
ingly dramatic pose, his hands were held high and clasped
tightly together, eyes gazing upward in what looked like
one supreme moment of ecstatic inspiration. That is the
Apostle Paul we prefer to imagine.

But the preconversion Paul (Saul) was never like that. In fact, he was probably not like that even after his experience of grace, as several scriptural flashes of temper indicate. For example, Paul worked himself into a lathering tirade while responding to the Galatians who were insisting that a man must be circumcised before becoming a Christian. The Revised Standard Version politely translates his poisonous rebut to the Galatians against the "circumcision party": "I wish those who unsettle you would mutilate themselves!" (Gal. 5:12). Paul more than hinted (in his original Greek sentence) that he wished those who advocated circumcision would go the whole way and just cut it *all* off! His response carries all the vituperative weight of suggesting that a modern-day Baptist who insists on total immersion should be drowned in the baptismal pool! As you can sense, Paul was a sassy apostle with a short fuse on a powder-keg temper!

Likewise Saul (preconversion Paul) was carried away on a holy mission: to exterminate Christianity. By his own admission, he was quite effective. Acts reports he went from house to house, arbitrarily seizing men and women alike, sending them to prison (Acts 8:1–3). Saul literally considered himself a "holy terror" and had managed to encase himself within a thick "safe" wall of piousness.

Yet Paul immediately continued in his letter to the Galatians, "But when he who had set me apart . . . and called me through his grace, was pleased to reveal his Son to me . . ." (Gal. 1:15–16). You are familiar with what happened at Paul's conversion: the voices from above, the blindness, the trip to the home of Ananias (Acts 9:1–19). The Galatians confession demonstrates

Paul's theological understanding of what happened: "But when he who set me apart . . . and called me through his grace . . ." Grace had summoned him out of his spiritual safe.

Imagine what a *surprise* this transformation would have been not only to Paul, but to all his colleagues, not to mention his Christian enemies! Paul, the Grand Inquisitor, *converted*? More than one person thought it a cunning ruse. What better way to infiltrate and destroy the enemy than to pose as a supplicant? Machiavelli and Torquemada would drool with envy at such a plan. On the other hand, former colleagues pursued Paul, too, and tried to execute him for treason. Paul was surrounded on all sides by people who found it hard to believe that grace had such surprising power.

Of course, Paul went on to forge a differing understanding of the Gospel, one that expanded God's grace to include the Gentiles, helping to make it unnecessary for them to follow the precepts of Jewish law before becoming followers of Christ. Actually, here Paul came to embrace the best of his religious heritage. For the religion of his preconversion behavior was perhaps not as faithful to his tradition as it seemed. Paul's Jewish heritage contained a rich tradition of love, mercy, and justice, as we will soon see. All Paul's writings reverberate with his radically surprising experience of grace in the context of his tradition:

> But now the righteousness of God has been manifested apart from law, although the law and the prophets bear witness to it, the righteousness of God through faith in Jesus Christ for all who believe. There is no distinction; since all have sinned and

fall short of the glory of God, they are justified by
his grace as a gift . . .

                                        Romans 3:21–24

For I am the least of the Apostles, unfit to be called
an apostle, because I persecuted the church of God.
But by the grace of God I am what I am, and his
grace toward me was not in vain. On the contrary,
I worked harder than any of them, though it was not
I, but the grace of God which is in me.

                                        1 Corinthians 15:9–10

And as we noted earlier with reference to Paul's "thorn
in the flesh":

Three times I besought the Lord about this, that it
should leave me, but he said to me, "My grace is
sufficient for you, for my power is made perfect in
weakness."

                                        2 Corinthians 12:8–9

The Apostle Paul's experience of grace has had a profound influence on Christians of every generation. St.
Augustine's *Confessions*—echoing Paul's rather tortured
path to Christ—reveals in splendid detail another saint's
warped and sordid path to surprising grace.

Augustine was born in northern Africa, in the year
354, to a "pagan" father and a devoutly Christian
mother. With agonizing honesty he chronicled his own
rebellion and sinfulness as a youth. He reflected at length
about having stolen a pear from a neighbor's yard. It
bothered him greatly, for he took the pear out of the sheer
joy of stealing—he didn't even *like* pears! Upon leaving

home for school as a young man he lived with a woman
out of wedlock with whom he had a son. (And we think
"living together" is a modern invention!) He became a
disciple of the Manichaean sect, believing in the equal
power of good and evil. Yet he could find no peace in
these beliefs. So he turned to philosophical Platonism as
a better answer to life's riddles—but his heart was still
not at rest.

At length and in beautifully crafted openness, Augustine tells how God entered his life unexpectedly. A great
preacher in the early church, Bishop Ambrose of Milan,
convinced him he could accept the Bible and the faith.
And in a surprising experience of conversion, Augustine
tells God of his blindness caused by a form of abundance
and of the grace that saved him:

> Too late came I to love You, beauty both so ancient
> and so fresh, yes too late came I to love you. And
> behold, You were within me, and I was out of my-
> self, where I looked for You: ugly, I rushed head-
> long upon those beautiful things You have made.
> You indeed were with me; but I was not with You:
> these beauties kept me far enough from You: even
> those, which unless they were in You, should not
> be as all. You called me and cried to me. You even
> broke open my deafness: Your beams shone on me,
> and You chased away my blindness . . . You touched
> me, and I burn again to enjoy Your peace.[7]

The lives of Paul and Augustine both indicate the surprising nature of God's about-face grace. (Some call this
repentance—and indeed it is, for to repent means simply
"to turn around.") Both saints experienced grace not as

an achievement but as a gift, not a stipend earned but a gracious offer made by God and accepted. Paul believed God had "called me through his grace." Augustine admitted, "You indeed were with me; but I was not with You." Neither found God. God found them.

Like many of us, they both tried to insulate themselves in abundance, though they were of different sorts. Paul cloaked himself in opulent overzealous piety, Augustine in physical delights and intellectual pride. Both were heavily encased in spiritual safes with little room for surprise. They had locked out grace.

Yet they were surprised by God's grace. In each of their lives God worked in unexpected ways. For Paul it was the humble piety of Stephen's noble martyrdom that confronted his own self-inflated holy terrorism. He was blinded so that he might see more clearly. For Augustine it was academic pride challenged by his intellectual equal Ambrose. Augustine's intellectual hubris was humbled only to be raised again, paradoxically making him one of the towering Christian intellects of history whose influence is still felt today. Subtly, God's grace jostled and even jolted both by confronting them with their own insulation from God. While both Paul and Augustine believed it could not have been otherwise (Augustine especially believed in the "irresistibility" of grace), the point is that God's grace pierced their encrusted armor of self-importance, confronting them with unforeseen self-knowledge and the gifts of forgiveness, courage, and the ability to change their lives radically.

To these two pilgrims on faith's journey, grace's surprises shattered their lives—only to provide even more grace to rebuild them upon another foundation. And that essential foundation is *openness* to receive God's grace as a free gift. It is not a commodity to be paid for, but a precious gift to accept humbly.

Therefore, Paul and Augustine grappled with the question that is our own: How can one who is insulated from surprise be surprised by grace? They both experienced the solution: allow yourself to be found by surprising grace.

Better To Give Than Receive—Or Is It?

There is a very simple examination you can give yourself to determine how well you may be able to accept grace and its surprises in your own life. Here's the test: When someone gives you a nice gift unexpectedly (aside from your birthday and other occasions when you may expect a gift), what is your first *emotional* response? Do you answer with something like, "Thank you very much for such a thoughtful gift," or do you reply, "But I didn't get *you* anything!"?

If your response is usually the latter, you probably also find it difficult to accept compliments or other kindnesses offered by friends or family members. If you feel this way, you are also not alone. Most of us have heard from earliest childhood, "It is better to give than receive." Of course, this is essential advice to children, who are prone toward selfishness and need to be taught the joys of giving. But is it *always* better to give than receive?

I once had an experience that made me reconsider the value not of giving but of receiving. A few years ago, I participated in a conference exploring issues of nuclear weapons and energy, attended by pastors, teachers, college students, and nuclear "experts." A world-renowned professor of nuclear engineering at a major university spoke about the need for all sectors of society to consider their interdependent needs which produce the demand for more complex and dangerous forms of nuclear technology. The chief problem with our society, he said, is that we tend to view ourselves as so independent and self-reliant that we cannot take advice from others or see our destiny as intimately intertwined with the future of others. We are so specialized, we see ourselves only by the uniqueness of what we can contribute, not by our inter-connectedness within a complex web of give-and-take relationships.

During an intermission after his speech, the professor was momentarily standing alone by a coffeepot. I decided to approach him to tell him how much I appreciated his words. As we chatted, he suddenly asked, "May I pour you a cup of coffee?"

"Thank you, no," I said politely, "I'll get it myself . . ."

The wise professor squinted his eyes at me and retorted sharply, "You tell me you liked my speech, but it appears you didn't hear a word I said! Here you and I stand, talking about our mutual interdependence, but you are so self-reliant that you will not even let me give you a little cup of coffee!"

He was absolutely correct! I had failed my own "grace test"! Rather than receive the gracious offer of a cup of coffee (which in my own mind meant I would owe him a kindness in return), I would rather do it myself and not owe anyone. In fact, the rejection of the professor's "gift" was an act of selfishness on my part. In a world where "It is better to give than to receive," the giver is always in a superior position to the receiver. And because I prefer to be superior rather than inferior to others, when

I refuse a gift it enables me to climb one rung higher on the superiority ladder.

Alone on top of a silly ladder is a quite lonely (and precarious) place to live, however. But that is where we dwell as long as we agree to accept gifts only when we have one to give in return.

As if the sage professor had not taught me this lofty lesson well enough, I had to learn it again not long afterward. This time the teacher was my sage five-year-old nephew, Ryan. Shortly before Christmas I was painting the dining room in my parents' new home with Ryan's "help." We were discussing all sorts of important things, like the sounds the letter *A* makes. Suddenly, Ryan smiled slyly at me and searched the room to see if anyone was around. We often play this game before we tell "secrets" to each other. When the "coast was clear," he whispered, "I've got a surprise for you."

"What do you mean?" I asked.

"I bought you a Christmas present *with my own money*. I picked it out *all by myself* and nobody knows what it is, not even Mommy!" he said with pride. (It's impossible to overemphasize the "with my own money" and "all by myself"!)

"How did you pull that off?"

"We had a special store at nursery school. High school boys and girls helped us pick out presents. I saved my money and got presents for Mommy and Daddy and Grandma and Grandpa and everybody." Never had I seen a brighter sparkle in his eyes.

Without thinking, I said to my nephew, "You shouldn't have done that, Ryan. You don't need to give me presents."

Striking my best Ben Franklinesque pose, I continued

the economics sermon: "You should save your money, son. Some day you'll need it for college. If you started saving a few dollars a month now, by the time you're ready for college, you'll have a tidy little sum collected. So why don't you save your money, okay?"

I would have made a great Puritan!

But Ryan's bubble of joy had visibly burst. He silently rushed away, almost in tears. When I caught up with him, I asked what was the matter. "But I *want* to give you my present. Don't you want my gift?"

Suddenly, I was standing self-reliant at the coffeepot again—only this time I had refused an even greater gift. Ryan's innocence had caught me off-guard and I reacted in my most natural manner—gracelessly. Rather than enjoy this precious moment when genuine affection was graciously expressed, I was not ready to accept the moment of surprise. Conversely, I actively worked against it. While I was able to patch things up with Ryan, I had blown a great opportunity—a delightful moment of surprising grace.

And how many gracious offers from God do we thoughtlessly discourage because we cannot receive surprising gifts graciously? For God's grace is itself a free gift, given unexpectedly, one that we did not and cannot earn or repay. As long as we swear by "It is better to give than receive," we will rarely be able to accept the surprises God's grace offers—even gifts offered through little children.

Administer the "grace test" to yourself. Chances are you are much like me—you have a difficult time receiving gifts graciously. But if we can learn to recognize and accept God's surprises, perhaps we will begin to see the many ways grace strikes us at unexpected moments every day.

That Stroke of Grace

Paul Tillich is a twentieth-century theologian who described what it means to accept grace in his famous sermon, "You Are Accepted." The words *sin* and *grace* sometimes sound strange to modern listeners because they are almost too well known, Tillich argued. To many people, they are shopworn words that have acquired distorted connotations caused by overuse. Tillich tried to convey the reality of ancient theological terms in a way accessible to modern thinkers while also faithful to the tradition that produced them. Therefore, Tillich talked about sin as "separation" or "estrangement," and grace as "acceptance" or "reconciliation." He wanted to wean us away from the simplicity of viewing sin as trifling misdeeds (pointing instead to the larger consequence of sin, which is separation from God and from our best selves), or regarding grace as nothing but easy forgiveness (advocating that grace is the larger reunion or reconciliation of God with humanity, humans with one another, and each of us with our own best selves).

Tillich quoted Paul's letter to the Romans: "Moreover the law entered, that the offense might abound. But where sin abounded, grace did much more abound" (Rom. 5:20). In this sense, sin and grace are bound to each other—one can have no knowledge of sin without knowledge of grace; that is, no knowledge of "acceptance" without the experience of "separation." Likewise, grace cannot be understood apart from sin, or the experience of separation apart from knowledge of acceptance.

True grace, according to Tillich, is not easy forgiveness, or a magical inner power standing outside one's everyday experience. Neither is grace mere benevolence or the gifts of nature or society. If any of these be grace alone, they are wistful and fleeting notions that quickly vanish under life's harsh vicissitudes:

> But grace is more than gifts. In grace something is overcome; grace occurs "in spite of" something; grace occurs in spite of separation and estrangement. Grace is the *re*union of life with life, the *re*conciliation of the self with itself. Grace is the acceptance of that which is rejected. Grace transforms fate into a meaningful destiny; it changes guilt into confidence and courage. There is something triumphant in the word "grace": in spite of the abounding of sin, grace abounds much more.[8]

When we have discussed being trapped in our spiritual safes, or feeling that we must pay our dues to God, we have been talking about the effects of sin, or "separation." And when we have talked about surprise, we have been discussing grace, or "acceptance." Hence Tillich, too, would speak of Paul's conversion: "The moment in which grace struck him and overwhelmed him, he was reunited with that to which he belonged, and from which he was estranged in utter strangeness." For Tillich's Paul, grace startled him within his unwitting alienation from God—ironically, precisely at the time when Paul thought he was closest to God. In that one stroke of grace, Paul was reconciled with God as well as with his own religious heritage. This transformation is indeed an astonishing miracle, especially for a terrorist!

Another modern person who described what it means to be surprised by grace was C. S. Lewis in his auto-biographical book, *Surprised by Joy*. There Lewis con-fessed his own pilgrimage from early adherence to Christianity to atheism, then conversion back to Chris-tianity. Like Paul and especially Augustine, Lewis's con-version was preceded by a long progression of events. Unlike the others, Lewis experienced no particularly dra-matic turnabout or a single explosive self-revelation. In-deed, the very lack of theatrics is part of what surprised Lewis. More profoundly, Lewis, too, experienced the confinement of the spiritual ''safe,'' though he described it differently:

> The odd thing was before God closed in on me, I
> was in fact offered what now appears a moment of
> wholly free choice . . . I became aware that I was
> holding something at bay, or shutting something out.
> Or, if you like, that I was wearing some stiff cloth-
> ing, like corsets, or even a suit of armor, as if I
> were a lobster. I felt myself being, there and then,
> given a free choice.[9]

Joy—God's grace—was wearing away his defenses. At first it meant becoming a theist. Then, subtly but surprisingly, joy conquered. It was not a lightning-bolt jolt, but more ''like when a man, after a long sleep, still lying motionless in bed, becomes aware that he is now awake.'' This quiet realization was how Lewis was ''sur-prised'' by joy: God's grace became gradually apparent, not miraculously revealed.

And this is the experience finally described by Tillich in the conclusion of his sermon on sin and grace. Tillich asked, "Do we know what it means to be struck by grace?" I hope by now you have sensed what it means. Indeed, to be "struck" by grace is to be surprised by its power to transform the humdrum. For grace is that power of God surprisingly bringing transformation, usually when we least expect it, and in ways we cannot foresee. As Tillich's epigraph to this chapter suggests, we cannot transform our own lives; only by the power of God's grace is that possible. Grace cannot be programmed, planned, or forced. But complacency, too, is the enemy of grace. Tillich reminds us grace strikes nevertheless:

> Grace strikes us when we are in great pain and restlessness. It strikes us when we walk through the dark valley of a meaningless and empty life. It strikes us when we feel that our separation is deeper than usual, because we have violated another life, a life which we loved, or from whom we were estranged. It strikes us when our disgust for our own being, our indifference, our weakness, our hostility, and our lack of direction and composure have become intolerable to us. It strikes when, year after year, the longed-for life does not appear . . . [10]

Sometimes our darkened spiritual safes are cracked open and the light of grace shines in. Only then may we know the meaning and surprise of grace. And then we can no longer ignore or be insulated from its penetrating power. Once we accept God's gracious offer of acceptance, we will no longer be the same.

So then surprising grace is that which startles us out of our attempts to be insulated from God. To be "struck by grace" is to be surprised by God's unexpectedness, the richness of comfort or the harshness of confrontation that ultimately transforms us in radical ways.

God's surprising grace penetrates our spiritual insulation in many seemingly mundane experiences. The best sermon I ever heard was like that. It was short and simple.

I was at a winter retreat one snowy February weekend. I must confess I was not getting much from the retreat, which was held during a particularly busy time for me. A mental checklist of pressing duties constantly swirled through my head like a blizzard. I was already looking forward to going home, where I could really get something accomplished! I was locked inside an inner world, allowing nothing to enter my ponderous isolation.

At about 10 P.M. on Saturday evening, our small group of fifteen bundled up in warm clothing and began trudging through knee-deep snow from our dormitory to the chapel some yards away. We were on our way to Compline, the bedtime prayer service taken from the medieval monastic tradition of daily prayers conducted at designated hours. With great difficulty we fought through the fresh snow toward the chapel. This is the last straw! I thought. I've got important things to do at home and here I am catching pneumonia going to pray! I seethed silently as the others chatted amiably.

Suddenly, in the middle of the woods separating our dorm from the chapel, our retreat leader stopped dead in his tracks. We found ourselves under a small streetlamp that lit the path to the chapel. The snow had left no trace of the sidewalk. Our leader just stood there in the dim light with his head reverently bowed. Much like stupid sheep we all halted, too, our tiny band of pilgrims bathed in a little swatch of white surrounded by darkness.

A curious hush came over our entire group as the

glistening snowflakes drifted down around us. After a moment, the stillness was pierced by the gentle voice of our retreat leader. With hands outstretched, he said simply, "Look around, God loves you."

Again, silence. The only movement was snowflakes whirling in the wind.

Immediately the tiny woods was transformed. I became lost in thought, transcending numb toes and frigid fingers. Forgotten were the pressing matters that had made me grumble. All that mattered at that moment were those words and this place. And I hadn't noticed what a glorious place it was! Fresh snow crystals sparkled in our tiny patch of light; but the circle of darkness surrounding us had its own mysterious charm. Shadows cast by the trees contrasted black and grey and white. The breeze sang a lonely muffled song through snow-heavy pine needles. Snowflakes melted into tears on my face as I watched hot breath vanish in the night air. Occasionally, the snow crunched softly as someone shifted weight from one foot to another. How precious and fragile life is, I thought, looking at the bundles of human warmth and creativity huddled together in the cold.

And those words, his five-word sermon. They were so much like this snowy scene, simple but laden with meaning. I chuckled to myself as I recalled the line in Robert Frost's poem: "And miles to go before I sleep." That's what I had thought rushing to Compline. But now nothing mattered more than thinking about this sermon of words and woods. Like the snowflakes randomly drifting on my face, all that had seemed so important melted on those grace-filled words. It is easy to lose track of God's love— like tracks in the snow eroded by a blustery wind, I

thought as I looked back on our disappearing trail from
the dorm.

We never made it to Compline. Or rather we had our
evening prayers standing solemnly in the woods. I am
grateful someone else had the sense to stop me in my
tracks that night—for a surprising gift of God's grace
was waiting there for those with sense enough to stop
and be found by it. Instantly my retreat was transformed
from one I considered meaningless to one that contained
a memorable moment of grace. When I reluctantly returned home, the chores that couldn't wait took on an
added dimension of meaning. I was surprised by how
different everyday life appeared after discovering grace
in the snowy woods.

It is hard to imagine how many other moments of
surprising grace I have missed as I grumble and trudge
my way through life, failing to look for surprises. I must
trample over many such moments: Many children have
given me gifts, but I remember only a few of them; I
have been offered gallons of coffee, but who did the
pouring?

God grants us much more grace than we have the
willingness to accept. It is like the story told by Doris
Donnelly about how her great-aunt Greta was given the
money to emigrate from Holland to America on an ocean
liner. Rather than travel in the more luxuriant upper
decks, she booked accommodations in the dank steerage
compartments of the ship's lower bowels. Upon leaving
Rotterdam a purser, sympathetic to the "huddled
masses" in steerage making their way to the New World,
graciously offered to allow several passengers from steerage the use of the upper decks. Many accepted the invitation and daily made their way topside. Because Greta

thought that the whole ship was like the dark and unpleasant lower compartments, she declined the offers to go up there.

When Greta finally arrived in New York she was surprised by what she had missed: The luxurious upper decks were festooned with chandeliers, richly carved wooden cornices, and long buffet tables filled with tasty foods and drinks. She then realized that her fellow fourth-class passengers had been enjoying these accommodations the whole journey while she languished below! "Imagine, it could have been mine, too, had I only said yes!"[11]

To many who are stranded in dark and dank compartments of spirituality, Donnelly says a gracious invitation is continually offered to us: "Friend, come up higher" (Luke 14:10). And while surprising treasures await those who accept this offer, some of us apprehensively lag behind, so comfortable in our discomfort that we fail to avail ourselves of what might become ours.

This story illustrates it may not only be abundance that insulates us from surprising grace. Indeed the overarching danger is *complacency* that refuses to risk openness. For the words of Jesus are true: "Seek and you shall find . . . Knock and the door shall be opened . . . Ask and it shall be given . . ." The fact that you are reading a book on grace proves you are already seeking, knocking, and asking. And you will be astounded at how much you will find as you continue to open yourself to God's surprising grace. In fact, you will be a-mazed.

CHAPTER III

A-mazing Grace—
"Grace That Comforts"

*"Grace" will not come because of any precision or because of
our mapping of a transcendent power. Graces will be found in
the mutually supportive relationality of the maze in which we
live—fraught with ambiguity and confusion and unexpected
twists and turns. As earth-creatures, we do not live in straight
lines; we truly do exist in a web, a network, a maze. Inter-
connectedness is the preeminent fact of the universe. When the
relationality is mutually supportive, and not distorted, we truly
can speak of "mazing grace."*[1]

—Larry Axel

*T*he mother paused momentarily in her weeping to blurt
out, "I always thought everything would work out if I
just tried hard enough. I tried to forgive my husband.
I've tried to forget it. I worked hard at making things
different than before. That's what they always say you're
supposed to do. But our marriage didn't work out, it got
worse.

"Why do people tell you forgiveness will make everything work out when it plainly doesn't?" she asked.

A reserved young business executive bitterly complained about the indignity done to him. "Why does my
boss think I've betrayed him? *He* was the one who was
having the affair with his secretary—the whole office
knew about it and she openly flaunted it. He could have
lost his job if the word got out! And when I thought I

52

should honestly tell him what it looked like to the others in the office, he accused *me* of spreading rumors about him, trying to undermine his authority. I acted out of *integrity*, trying to help him, and he reacted with para-noia and vengeance! Talk about beheading the messen-ger. Now *I* have to quit or be fired because his superiors believe that I caused the trouble! My whole family is going to suffer because I only did what was right.

"Why do people like that win?" he asked.

The terminally ill cancer patient wheezed out a wry laugh as he pointed out to me the "get well" cards taped to the wall of his hospital room. "Greeting card com-panies don't make any to give to someone who's dying. I've thought up a few cards, though. How about this: The outside of the card has one of those big yellow smiley faces and when you open it up it says, 'Have a Nice Death!' " I grinned but he suddenly grew serious. "You know, out of all the people who have come in here not one of my friends has mentioned the fact I'm going to die. They act like I don't know.

"Why is it so hard for my friends to talk with me about death?" he asked.

Hard questions all.

Life in the Maze

Queries and circumstances like these three remind us that fitting and truthful answers to life's vexing questions are hard to come by. Those who once believed the bed-time fairy-tale ending "And they all lived happily ever after," are rudely awakened from their carefree slumber

when confronted by situations they can neither understand nor control. Philosopher David Hume long ago
observed about our limits of understanding, ''The whole
is a riddle, an inexplicable mystery. Doubt, uncertainty,
suspense of judgment appear the only results of our most
accurate scrutiny concerning this subject.''

Many aspects of our lives are clouded by ambiguity,
bewilderment, perplexity. Fairy-tale endings are little but
wishful thinking. Far from a tidy ''happily ever after,''
life as we experience it is more like a riddle, a puzzle,
a labyrinth—a *maze*.

Mazes have been around for thousands of years. Ancient cultures all over the world have used the labyrinth
as a symbol for life's oftentimes twisted search for a
central meaning. We are most familiar with the ancient
use of mazes from the Greek myth that told of Daedalus,
an architect, who designed a labyrinth to house the
half-human, half-bull beast called the Minotaur. Some
Greek cities were even constructed as mazes in order to
confuse and ambush invading soldiers. Archaeologists
have found forms of mazes used for religious rites in
places as far apart as Egypt, Scandinavia, and Southeast
Asia.

More recently, labyrinths have been used for sport.
Majestic royal palace grounds throughout Europe are
strewn with well-manicured hedge mazes, a remnant of
more glorious days. You've no doubt seen the paintings
of richly clothed eighteenth-century monarchs gaily
prancing about in their perfectly landscaped gardens.
These regnant lords, well insulated from the uncompro-
mising realities of life forced upon their subjects by royal
extravagance, could afford to make fun of confusion.

We have similar versions of the maze in our own day

as well: The House of Mirrors at the amusement park offers us the chance to be playfully confused by contorted images of ourselves as we try to make our way out into the light of day. Even in modern Japan, one of the most popular recreational pastimes among the well-to-do is the so-called "maze craze." Japanese families buy admission tickets to enter any number of mazes for the pleasure of trying to find their way out. For those who become helplessly frustrated, however, conspicuously marked emergency exits are scattered throughout the labyrinth, allowing one to "call off" the game if it becomes overwhelming.

Of course, there are no easy emergency exits in real labyrinthine existence. Rather than neat, well-trimmed rows of hedges, the periphery of the *real* maze is guarded by troublesome nettles, thorns, and thistles. Life's mazing actualities offer more hardship than merriment.

If we are truly honest with ourselves, we must admit that we often experience bewilderment. Ernest Hemingway often wrote of the hopelessness that can arise from this recognition. In *A Farewell to Arms*, the narrator, Frederic Henry, flees war to avoid death and suffering only to find himself ironically facing the death of his lover and their child. In an anguished moment of reflection near the end of the story, the despondent Henry recalls an experience on a camping trip before the war:

Once in camp I put a log on top of the fire and it was full of ants. As it commenced to burn, the ants swarmed out and went first toward the centre where the fire was; then turned back and ran toward the end. When there were enough on the end they fell off into the fire. Some got out, their bodies burnt

and flattened, and went off not knowing where they
were going. But most of them went toward the fire
and then back toward the end and swarmed on the
cool end and finally fell off into the fire. I remember
thinking at the time that it was the end of the world
and a splendid chance to be a messiah and lift the
log off the fire and throw it out where the ants could
get off onto the ground. But I did not do anything
but throw a tin cup of water on the log, so that I
would have the cup empty to put whiskey in before
I added water to it.

The passage contains striking symbolic allusions to
God's seeming indifference and antlike human futility.
Hemingway's literary theologizing, through the character
Henry, reaches its climax with this mocking cosmic pun:
"I think the cup of water on the burning log only steamed
the ants."[2]

Absorption with despair devoid of hope can lead some,
as it did with Hemingway himself, to consider suicide
as the only "emergency exit" from the maze.

Other people, also bewildered by the hazy mysteries
of life, refuse to admit the network of ambiguity they
live in. Failure to acknowledge life's enigmas can result
in spiritual, psychological, and emotional damage. Well-
meaning but ill-informed people try to paper over the
confounding and sometimes contradictory aspects of
being human, often for what they think are religious
reasons. "Faith," this type of person asserts, "ought
only to *answer* questions, provide only clarity. Every
random event, every indiscriminate deed, has a perfect
explanation in relation to God's 'will.'" Therefore, according to this vantage point, when confronted with any

ambiguity or frustration, any painful experience or grief, one simply resigns to "Let go and let God." Never do such people admit confusion or doubt or questions. Perhaps, because their searching and questions are so limited, neither does their spiritual life nor their comprehension of God's grace have much depth.

For these people the "happily ever after" syndrome is what faith ought to provide them. Unlike the "Hemingways" who are so enmeshed in the ambiguity that they fail to find any hope within the maze, "happily ever after" folks can never quite entertain ambiguity and thereby an avenue of an important element of grace.

They are somewhat like the subjects of the following psychological study. Two psychologists stacked an otherwise normal deck of playing cards with incongruous cards of their own creation, such as a red six of spades or a black four of hearts. They flashed the cards before their subjects and asked them to identify them. With only a brief time to see each card, at first every person identified the anomalous card incorrectly. Later, when given a longer time to observe each card, most people realized which cards were incongruent and could afterward quickly identify the "ringers." However, the researchers noted, "A few subjects . . . were never able to make the requisite adjustment of their categories. Even at forty times the average exposure required to recognize normal cards for what they were, more than 10 percent of the anomalous cards were not correctly identified. And the subjects who then failed often experienced acute personal distress. One of them exclaimed: 'I can't make the suit out, whatever it is. It didn't even look like a card that time. I don't know what color it is now or whether it's

a spade or a heart. I'm not even sure now what a spade
looks like. My God!' ''[3]

Riddles And Religion

When we must confront the confusing complexities of
life, our response is often, ''My God!'' Riddles give rise
to religion. For as we have discovered, the maze is a
symbol in many cultures and religions of the religious
search for meaning. And the labyrinth as a symbol for
the journey of the soul toward God also has a rich heritage
in the Christian faith. Many medieval cathedrals incorporated labyrinths into their architecture. The greatest
cathedrals of Europe—Chartres, Reims, Amiens, probably Notre Dame in Paris, and maybe even Coventry—all contained mosaic mazes built into the floor of
the nave.

Medieval mazes served a dual purpose. At a secondary
level, the maze was used by the master builder of a
cathedral as a sort of signature piece—the architect in-
scribed his name at the heart of the labyrinth (echoing
the mythical architectural originator of the maze, Daedalus). In time, the cathedral maze even became known
as the *Maison de Dalus* (''House of Daedalus'').

But the medieval maze also had a serious religious
function. The cathedral nave labyrinth was above all used
as a form of penance. A penitent who had come to the
church seeking forgiveness and guidance would sometimes crawl or walk through the maze, tracing the twisting
route of stone engraved on the floor of the cathedral nave.
Since the center of the maze also represented the presence
of God (and the twists and turns of the maze signified

the difficult journey to Jerusalem or heaven), the penitential trek through the labyrinth was seen as a mini-pilgrimage, a humble and holy search for God amid the twisted and confusing circumstances that had compelled the pilgrim to seek divine guidance from the church.

Isn't it fascinating that Christians from ages past (who often spent over a hundred years constructing these magnificent cathedrals) would build *confusion* into their chief religious monuments? Perhaps they possessed a degree of wisdom that is lost on our generation. Maybe they understood better than we that if we are truly to rebuild our lives by grace we must allow God to assist us even in our mazelike confusions. Only by exploring the riddles of life may we unlock religion's deeper meanings.

Over ten years of serving as a pastor has taught me that any family or individual can be suffering an inward whirlwind of bewilderment, but outwardly appear quite placid. Middle- and upper-class people are generally very proficient at masking their confusions and questions. Church people are often the very best at denying difficulties, even though we profess candor about our weaknesses. We sometimes prefer to put on a mask of piety and "play church," rather than bare our deepest fears and insecurities to one another in genuine love and acceptance. But when we move beyond this easy simplicity and recognize our moral and spiritual complexities, God's grace can begin to rebuild new areas of our lives that have remained untouched for years.

This was the case with a gentleman I once knew who burst into my study at church late one afternoon. He was a respected member of the community, the very picture of prosperity and integrity. He attended worship services regularly with his family, was an able leader, and lived in a fine neighborhood. Only the day before we had exchanged polite greetings and smiles. Now he stormed into my office, disheveled and absolutely beside himself. He plopped into a chair and, leaning forward with his elbows resting on his knees and his face buried in his hands, he began to sob.

"I've just gotta get something off my chest. I'm so confused I just can't stand it anymore," he cried out.

Astonished at the sight of this usually dignified man in total disarray, I came around my desk, sat in the chair beside his, and wrapped my arm around him in consolation. Immediately, he fell to his knees, took my hand, and held it to his wet cheek as he wept wildly.

"I've embezzled some money where I work," he finally stammered. "God, I don't know how it happened. At first, it was just a few dollars—I meant to pay it back! Then it was more and more. Nobody ever noticed."

"*Did* someone notice? Is that why you're here?" I asked.

"No, but I don't know what to do! God, I want to give it back, but it's so much money now I can't return it without admitting what I did! What will happen then? I'd be arrested, fired! My family, our friends! God! How did this happen!"

Never have I seen anyone more distressed; and seldom had I ever witnessed a more striking contrast than the calm man who greeted me yesterday and this troubled soul writhing on the floor now. He was caught in a trap of his own making. The outward placidity of his life was only a ruse designed to fool other people (and God). He sincerely wanted help and to amend his dishonesty. But his foot was caught in the door of genteel respectability:

He couldn't correct the wrong he had committed without admitting he was a fraud.

There are complex psychological, social, and spiritual forces that contribute to generally respectable persons committing disreputable acts. It is much like when an innocent stroll through the forest turns into a nightmare of panic if you lose your sense of direction. And when elaborate circumstances involving self-deception, dishonesty, and ignorance lead us into immorality or spiritual confusion, the only path to God is sometimes the way of the maze.

And through the maze was the only way out for this troubled man. After several days of tortured soul-searching, he decided that he must admit the theft to his boss and suffer the consequences. Before he went to confess, we knelt together at the altar of the church and he prayed for forgiveness and strength.

Because he freely admitted his crime, his employer graciously agreed to let him return the money along with his resignation, on the condition he seek professional therapy. When he told his family and several close friends what had happened, they were devastated. But he told them he could not keep lying to himself and to them any longer.

Soon he found a job in another city and, through therapy, came to understand some of the dynamics in his background that had caused the problem. Before he left town, he again visited my study. He was calm this time— but it was not the false peace he harbored before this experience in the maze.

"I still don't fully understand what happened to me— or why I didn't have to go to jail. I'm still working on that. But even though this had been the most bewildering time of my life, I've never felt so close to God."

Until now he had been looking me straight in the eye. But now he lowered his head, saying, "And even though God knows I am . . ."

After a long choked pause he looked up again and with quivering lips whispered, "And even though God knows I am . . . a fraud, somehow I've never felt more at peace."

In many ways it is a shame that we no longer have mazes in our churches to crawl through in order to remind us that life's journey is more like wandering a maze than running straight through a 100-yard dash. Built-in labyrinths in our churches would remind us that God's grace is not only found along cheerful primrose paths but on twisted, meandering mazes of confusion and doubt.

Wrestling With Ambiguity

To paraphrase Tolstoy, some questions are asked not that we might answer them but that we might spend our whole life wrestling with them. The problem we cannot avoid is that when we grapple with hard questions we sometimes come away from our wrestling match limping. However, even in limping away we discover a blessed event has occurred, as did Jacob after his bout with the "angel" in Genesis 32.

The Bible is crystal clear about at least one thing: Jacob was among the greatest all-time con artists. The Book of Genesis (beginning with chapter 27) tells how Jacob charmingly deceived his father, cheated his brother, jousted in dishonesties with his uncle/father-in-law-twice-over Laban (which made Jacob quite a wealthy cheat), and often approached God with unbelievable effrontery. Oddly, however, even amid his morally questionable shenanigans, Jacob continually sought God and was granted sublime visions of God's glory and promise (see the stories of Bethel, Gen. 28:10ff, 35:9ff—the first is the "Jacob's ladder" vision).

Midway through Jacob's story in Genesis is his weird wrestling match. Jacob had been up to his usual antics—in the dead of night he had just fled Haran with much of his father-in-law's possessions. He was hotly pursued by Laban, but the two soon kissed and made up. Jacob's charm was still holding out. But as he came nearer to home he began to fear his brother's retribution. After all, Jacob had swindled Esau out of his rightful inheritance. So Jacob sent ahead lavish gifts to soften Esau's wrath. As the confrontation drew nearer, his apprehension intensified. Just before the showdown, Jacob sent away his wives and children to a safe place and was finally left alone. Then the bell sounded in Round One of Jacob's bout with God's a-mazing grace.

The Bible is a bit fuzzy as to the actual identity of Jacob's wrestling partner. The match was fierce, lasting all night. It seems bizarre that the two could wrestle until daybreak with no victor, especially since all the visiting opponent finally had to do was lightly touch Jacob's thigh to put it out of joint. Nevertheless, Jacob secured a "blessing" from the anonymous stranger. The wrestler then disappeared as mysteriously as he appeared.

The text says Jacob named that place "Penuel" ("the face of God") because he said he had seen God face-to-face. The vignette concludes, "The sun rose upon him as he passed Penuel, limping because of his thigh . . ." (Gen. 32:32).

What are we to make of this outlandish story? One

overriding picture of Jacob emerges from these scenes: a person who, despite his innumerable shortcomings, harbored an unquenchable desire to understand how God was a part of his life. Jacob's magnificent visions represent a profound yearning for God to clarify and purify his confusion. Yet God's presence could mean no simple blessing of Jacob's avarice and malice. And so Jacob wrestled with the ambiguity of his own labyrinthine life, an existence filled both with lying and love for God, cheating and charity, haughtiness and humility. When the match was over, Jacob sorely staggered away. But his limping was blessed.

This symbolic story contains several lessons, including one about grace. As Frederick Buechner has written:

Another part of the lesson was that, luckily for Jacob, God doesn't love people because of who they are but because of who he is. *It's on the house* is one way of saying it and *it's by grace* is another, just as it was by grace that it was Jacob of all people who became not only the father of the twelve tribes of Israel but the many times great grandfather of Jesus of Nazareth, and just as it was by grace that Jesus of Nazareth was born into this world at all.[4]

It is an example of *a-mazing* grace that the old rascal Jacob found God's blessing mingled with his morally chequered life. God did not condone Jacob's charlatanry. Rather, Jacob found grace wrestling with the mundane in his tangled life of good and evil. It was a gift freely given him at an anxious moment. In these contrasting circumstances, only by grace could he be both so blessed and remain such a scoundrel.

It would be a nice "happily ever after" ending to the Jacob story to say he limped away a thoroughly changed man, thereafter leading a spotless life. That didn't happen. But Jacob was changed nonetheless. He was altered not because he had adopted higher ethical standards or had decided by sheer willpower to be more devoted or faithful. He was touched by that unexpected "stroke of grace," the surprising gift of God that rather painfully wrestled its way into his ambiguous life. Grace was given him within his serpentine trail.

In the Belly Of A Paradox

Another of the many biblical stories that speaks to this grace amid ambiguity is the story of Jonah. Jonah, like many of us, was a character who vaguely wanted to do what was right, decided to swim in the opposite direction, then quite unwittingly found himself in an uncomfortable quandary!

The opening three verses of the book of Jonah initiate us into this "prophet's" dilemma:

Now the word of the Lord came to Jonah the son of Amittai, saying, "Arise, go to Nineveh, that great city, and cry against it; for their wickedness has come up before me." But Jonah rose to flee to Tarshish from the presence of the Lord. He went down to Joppa and found a ship going to Tarshish; so he paid the fare, and went on board, to go with

them to Tarshish, away from the presence of the
Lord.

Jonah 1:1–3

Any halfway decent former Sunday school student
knows the next episode. Jonah's shipmates fed our anti-
hero to the sea, and the "great fish" obliged God's purpose. The parable continues with Jonah's lamenting psalm
of confusion from the belly of the great "fish":

> I called to the Lord in my distress,
>   and he answered me;
> out of the belly of Sheol I cried
>   for help,
>   and thou hast heard my cry.
> Thou didst cast me into the depths,
>   far out at sea,
>   and the flood closed round me;
>   all thy waves, all thy billows, passed over me.
> I thought I was banished from thy sight
>   and should never see thy holy temple again.
> The water about me rose up to my neck;
>   the ocean was closing over me.
> Weeds twined about my head
>   in the troughs of the mountains;
>
> I was sinking into a world
>   whose bars would hold me fast for ever.

Jonah 2:2–6 (NEB)

This image of Jonah's pitiful bellyaching contrasts
sharply with the courage of the patriarchal warriors
(Joshua or Caleb) or the "blood and guts" prophets like

Amos, Jeremiah, and Isaiah (whom we will discuss in chapter 4). Jonah was no obedient leatherneck marine willing to salute smartly and conquer any military target the Lord ordered. He was a recalcitrant laughingstock, not even as obedient to the Lord's command as the huge sea creature. But this is not the last of Jonah's ironies.

You recall that the fish dutifully vomited Jonah up at the Assyrian capital. There, evangelist Jonah's brief but highly successful "Nineveh Crusade" confirms he was only a reluctant participant in God's graceful purpose. But Jonah was not finished complaining. By the time the Ninevites finally repented, Jonah had had a bellyful of God's goodness. Jonah chastised God: "I knew that thou art a gracious God and merciful, slow to anger, and abounding in steadfast love . . ." (4:2). Imagine! God had shown mercy to the detestable Assyrians, not punished them! Rather than respond with empathy or relief, Jonah was so confused and embittered he asked God to take his life. Better to be at peace by death than to endure this bewildering paradox: God had managed to grace Nineveh even through an unwitting coward!

Jonah sulked in perplexity, showing more remorse over the loss of his shade tree than the lostness of Nineveh. And so the book of Jonah concludes, the only book of the Bible to end with a question. In essence the Lord asks: Does Jonah care more about a mere plant than the mass of humanity in Nineveh God wants to bless? It is a question that causes us to ponder God's presence in a world confused by hatred, suffering, and division. Jonah's entire contradictory career begs this question.

The ever-insightful Thomas Merton hit upon the book of Jonah's meaning when he wrote:

I have had to accept the fact that my life is almost
totally paradoxical. I have also had to learn gradually
to get along without apologizing for the fact, even
to myself. And perhaps this preface is an indication
that I have not yet completely learned. No matter.
It is in the paradox which was and is still a source
of insecurity, that I have come to find the greatest
security. I have become convinced that the very
contradictions in my life are in some ways signs of
God's mercy to me; if only because someone so
complicated and so prone to confusion and self-
defeat could hardly survive for long without special
mercy.[5]

Merton named this "sign of God's mercy to me," in the
title of a book, *The Sign of Jonas*, which he wrote because
"like Jonas himself I find myself travelling toward my
destiny in the belly of a paradox."[6]

What an apt description of Jonah's predicament (and
ours too!). At the same time, what an affirmation of
Jonah's experience of grace. Grace appeared to Jonah
not as some colossal disclosure, not as a lofty revelation
bringing crystal clarity to a muddled mess. Grace was
hardly a reward for Jonah's courageous faithfulness. No,
grace came to Jonah clothed in contradiction, paradox,
irony. His zigzag devotion mattered not. God's mercy
was shown in spite of Jonah's floundering resolve. Despite Jonah's reluctance, he found himself "travelling
toward his destiny in the belly of a paradox." And so
God's probing question, and Jonah's confounding career,
both direct us to a provisional answer to our question:
Where is God in the maze? God is present within the
maze, paradoxically participating in the confusion while

at the same time adding a measure of meaning to it.

This is not so much an "answer" to the question as it is a paradoxical affirmation of faith about God. In this way a paradox differs significantly from a contradiction. A contradiction is the logical incompatibility of two ideas or things which cannot be reconciled. The first Epistle of John reveals the incompatible contradiction of saying you love God while hating your neighbor (I John 2:1–6; 4:20–21).

On the other hand, a paradox is found when two seemingly contradictory ideas in reality together express a higher truth. An excellent example of a paradox is when Jesus said, "He who finds his life will lose it, and he who loses his life for my sake will find it" (Matt. 10:39; also see Luke 17:33). It is a logical contradiction to say you will find your life by giving it away. (Jesus was speaking in this context about "picking up your cross" to follow him.) But the transcending truth is that as long as all your everyday concerns are only for your own self and happiness, contentment will be elusive. Yet when you offer your life in love for someone or something greater than yourself, then you mysteriously (and paradoxically) find the happiness and contentment you were seeking to begin with.

Both contradiction and paradox contain a tension between conflicting ideas. But the stress found within a paradox can lead to a deeper insight about the nature of tension itself. Thus the tension created by attempting to discern God's presence in the perplexing maze is an exercise in paradox. Affirming God's grace in life's maze may seem contradictory: How can God be present when we are so confused by beguiling situations? Yet experience and faith teach that God's steadfast love is often found in lives riddled with puzzlement. Maybe the tensions of contradiction, paradox, and pain are not to be easily resolved. Perhaps paradoxical tension forces us to dig a deeper spiritual well into which we might lower our bucket of despair and find a fresher source of well-being. In the words of Parker Palmer, echoing Thomas Merton, "Perhaps one could be swallowed up by paradox and still be delivered to the shores of one's destiny—even as was Jonah from the belly of the whale." [7]

Comfort Within the Uncomfortableness

Jonah's story is a tale of "a-mazing grace." It is grace that appeared unexpectedly, surprisingly. But it was *not* the grace given to understand. A-mazing grace is that which enables us to no longer deny life's agonizing tensions, the terror of the unknown, the torment of loss, the frustration of incompleteness, the ache of loneliness, the emptiness of plenty. It is grace that enables us to accept somehow the hardships no one can adequately explain. Grace is the tender, freely given caress of a God who suffers, too.

Long ago the idea that God suffers for and with us was condemned as a heresy. This belief—called Patripassianism (which means "The Suffering of the Father," or the idea that God the Father suffered as Jesus the Son was crucified)—was rejected because the early church leaders believed it did not adequately differentiate between Jesus and God as distinct members of the Trinity. More recently, however, many theologians have begun to rethink the wisdom of affirming that indeed God suffers with us. While there may be comfort in the notion that God is an entirely powerful far-off figure in charge of every minute detail of the universe, there is also a great deal of comfort in the idea that God's grace need not solve all problems or resolve all tensions.

Frankly, for reasons only God understands, some pieces to the puzzle will never fit. But grace allows the puzzle to remain incomplete. Some problems maintain more integrity unsolved, just as some tensions yield more meaning unresolved. At the same time, this puzzling grace does not leave us bereft of comfort or care. For there is great comfort in the idea that God does not spare us from the suffering in which God is willing to participate as well.

This search for comfort has another implication in the Jonah story. Jonah's stubborn frustration was the result of his unwillingness to look beyond his own immediate needs. He was so stiffened by his protective armor in the battle with paradox he was not capable of sharing himself with needy humans under his care. He had successfully "looked out for number one," but his searching and isolation left him only angry and empty.

Life has a dimension much larger than our own individual experience of it. We belong to communities, organizations, churches, clubs, support groups, gatherings of friends—the list is infinite. We are part of a network of other people who are at times confused just like us, whether they admit it or not. Others share the same triumphs and tragedies we do. We are not alone.

But sometimes groups of people are part of our problem. Communities of imperfect human beings cannot be governed without friction and conflict. Friendship's openness necessitates clashing opinions. Churches must wrangle over building blueprints and children's gooey fingerprints messing up sacred walls. We are all bundles of contradictions jostling with one another to understand and to be understood. Some of our most treacherous journeys are into the twisted and misunderstood hearts of other human beings.

Worse, real evil bedevils us. Buchenwald, "Gulag Archipelago," Cambodia, South Africa, and Hiroshima quickly conjure up a comprehension of the human capacity for evil and destruction. Hatred, oppression, discrimination, disease, and tragedies all can ruin any sense of security we might feebly construct. The sheer messiness of the human heart challenges any Pollyanna optimism about human nature.

Yet it is into this messiness that God has come to demonstrate that even in darkness, grace is present. "Even the darkness is not dark to thee," says Psalm 139.

In what I believe is one of the most moving passages in all literature, Nobel Laureate Elie Wiesel, in his autobiographical memoir, *Night* (about his years in Nazi death camps), tells of this Presence and absence even in the dark death of an innocent child:

> One day when we came back from work, we saw three gallows rearing up in the assembly place, three black crows. Roll call. SS all round us, machine guns trained: the traditional ceremony. Three victims in chains—and one of them, the little servant, the sad-eyed angel.
>
> The SS seemed more preoccupied, more disturbed than usual. To hang a boy in front of thousands of spectators was no light matter . . .
>
> The three victims mounted together onto the chairs.

The three necks were placed at the same moment within the nooses.

"Long live liberty!" cried the two adults.

But the child was silent.

"Where is God? Where is He?" someone behind me asked. At a sign from the head of the camp, the three chairs tipped over.

Total silence throughout the camp. On the horizon, the sun was setting.

"Bare your heads!" yelled the head of the camp. His voice was raucous. We were weeping.

"Cover your heads!"

Then the march past began. The two adults were no longer alive . . . But the third rope was still moving; being so light, the child was still alive. . . .

For more than half an hour he stayed there, struggling between life and death, dying in slow agony under our eyes. And we had to look him full in the face . . .

Behind me, I heard the same man asking:

"Where is God now?"

And I heard a voice within me answer him:

"Where is He? Here He is—He is hanging here on this gallows. . . ."[8]

This moment should do nothing less than *gnaw* on the soul. This image, and the larger Holocaust of which it is a part, must never be forgotten and must forever be deplored as a crime against all humanity. Yet even standing before an unspeakable and utterly senseless sight, such as the execution of a boy, *something* still points to the horror and dares to whisper into the abyss, "There God is . . . There I *am* . . ." As confounding as it seems, solidarity and connectedness with other humans in the midst of misery is where God's a-mazing presence is acutely felt. Again, ours is not a grace to *understand* why our world (or God) allows such indignity to exist. It is a simple suffering grace that imperfectly remains present in our unresolved tensions and in our unsolved confusion, a grace that helps us find comfort not in our refusal to face facts nor in simplistic answers to cosmic riddles. It is grace to face the hard, concrete, excruciatingly painful realities of the maze with paradoxical mixtures of courage and cowardice, hurt and hope, dejection and daring, absence and Presence.

A-mazing grace is comfort that consoles us within our uncomfortableness.

Comforting The Afflicted: Forgiveness, Friendship, And Hope

If indeed grace "inflicts the comfortable" as we will shortly learn, a-mazing grace "comforts the afflicted." The most important avenue for this grace is through the joy and messiness of human relationships. Solidarity with others caught in the paradoxical web helps us understand we do not need to resolve the unresolvable single-handedly. In community with others we learn how friends handle conflicts, how churches find communion in chaos, how friction can bear forgiveness. Through mutual support and openness, we learn how graceful hope can foster "comfort within our uncomfortableness." Indeed, forgiveness, friendship, and hope—these are a few ways grace consoles those who search for meaning within the uncomfortable maze.

FORGIVENESS

   Sooner or later, the tensions of living in the maze cause conflicts. Self-interests collide. Carelessness breeds tragedy. Ballooned expectations deflate. Effective communication falters. Motives are misunderstood. All these strains and many more sometimes cause us pain and shame. Because we hurt, we in turn injure others. The pain created by confused human interaction is indeed one of the major sources of our distress. Nothing is more dazing than the grinding friction of intransigent human wills locked in conflict.

   The result of these frictions are acts of harm we inflict on one another. Whether intentional or not, damage is perpetrated when complexity and anxiety fray nerves and create conflict and discomfort. Astonishing amounts of hate and anger can fester between people even over slight differences. Neighbors bicker over inches in property boundary disputes. Families fight over pennies of inheritance. The day after Christmas transforms the season's good cheer into surly shoppers at department store "return" windows!

   Worse still, frightening individual and institutional evils can mushroom by the commonplace complacency of everyday people who refuse to act. We often read in the newspaper of chilling crimes (like a mugging or rape) committed openly in public with scores of people quickly passing by, afraid to act or intercede for fear of "getting involved." Tillich was correct: Modernity creates conditions where conflict produces "alienation" and "estrangement." And with these tensions comes the accompanying yearning for reconciliation, reunion, and forgiveness—grace—to assist us in navigating all the dangerous twists and turns in the maze we must face.

We must learn to practice forgiveness if we are to survive in this world. We are not discussing divine forgiveness, God's mercy toward our sinfulness. Rather, our forgiveness toward other humans ultimately flows from divine forgiveness—and is at best only a pale reflection of it. Human forgiveness is pardon that attempts to forgive not from a herculean act of the will, but from an honest recognition of our mutual containment in the complex, conflicting, and confounding web of life.

You've no doubt read and heard many inspiring stories of magnanimous forgiveness, how the parents of a child killed by a drunk driver "forgave" him because things just weren't going his way lately. On the surface these stories appear to be glowing and unbelievable examples of an almost inhuman willpower to "forgive." But I must confess many of these stories leave me rather unsatisfied, and, frankly, skeptical. They seem almost as if the righteous victims inflict "forgiveness" like a weapon upon the wrongdoer, as if it were in their power and duty to wipe the slate totally clean, to "forgive and forget" even the most hideous deeds with a careless emotional about-face. Notwithstanding the appearance of forgiveness, many (but not all) of these warm narratives tell not of the *ability* to forgive. Rather, they mask the refusal to recognize honestly the nature of their painful puzzle and how a devastating twist in the maze has confronted them. They practice not inhuman forgiveness but a subtle form of inhumane vengeance. It is as if the wronged says to the wrongdoer, "You have hurt me terribly and caused an irreparable void in my life, and I will punish you by torturing your conscience with my superiority. I will 'forgive' you, for that is what I must do to preserve my ascendancy over you. I still hate you, only now my hate is disguised as righteousness.'' Of course, these thoughts and actions are quite unconscious—and if confronted with these feelings, they would deny in the strongest terms that they truly feel this way. But this kind of "forgiving" only masks a warped religious vow never to forgive.

This condescending attitude prevails not only in tragic circumstances where in fact there *is* much to forgive, but also in everyday interaction. A friend of mine once had a colleague at work who imagined my friend had convinced others to dislike him. (The colleague didn't need anyone persuading others to dislike him, he accomplished that quite well on his own.) Despite my friend's denials, the colleague's paranoid suspicions persisted as he spread lies about the disloyalty. Finally, after my friend thought the matter was forgotten, the coworker announced he had "forgiven" him!

Few things are more annoying than being "forgiven" for something you didn't do. But how can you argue with someone who has "forgiven" you? This false forgiveness is what Thomas Merton meant when he wrote of spiritual pride, "This sickness is most dangerous when it succeeds in looking like humility. When a proud man thinks he is humble his case is hopeless."[9] The corresponding danger is when proud hatred is convinced it is "forgiving."

Equally troublesome is a bystander offering cheap forgiveness for a crime committed against someone else. A storm of controversy erupted in 1985 when President Reagan visited the Bitburg cemetery, burial place of several SS soldiers who had participated in the Nazi death camps. One letter to our local newspaper suggested Reagan's visit trivialized the Holocaust, demeaning events like the tragedy described by Elie Wiesel. Another

well-meaning but ill-informed letter suggested that the
Holocaust *should* be forgotten; "Forgive and forget" the
writer argued. Several other angry letters denounced such
shallow forgiveness. One made a particularly telling
point: It was not the writer's place to suggest that others
should forgive a crime that did not harm her. Brutality
can only be "forgiven" by the one whom it has hurt.
To "forget" atrocity in the name of cheap forgiveness
is not only unwise, it is un-Christian.

Please don't misunderstand these examples: I am not
advocating that we should "blame the victim" (or ourselves) when a wrong is committed. I am suggesting that
when we attempt to "forgive" the wrongs committed
against us (or others) within the maze we ought to consider carefully what true forgiveness means. Forgiveness
is not an *ability* or a spiritual achievement gained by a
teeth-gritting act of the will. Forcing yourself to "forgive" when you desire not to is both masochistic and
sadistic: You harm yourself because you have not touched
true human forgiveness and you have harmed another by
inflicting further punishment on an already guilty party.
Feigning forgiveness robs both the wronged and the
wrongdoer of working through a much needed process
toward healing and true human forgiveness.

In his excellent book, *Forgive and Forget*, Lewis
Smedes recommends three steps toward human forgiveness: hurt, hate, and healing.[10] When someone wrongs
you it *hurts*, and to "forget it" is not only unjust, it is
unhealthy. Without truly feeling the hurt, it is not possible
to move onward toward healing.

The same is true with the next aspect of forgiveness,
hate. Too often hate is interpreted as contrary to proper
religiosity—and in fact when carried too far, or when

founded on injustice, ignorance, or discrimination, hate *is* evil. But there is a *righteous* hatred, a loathsome aversion to evil that is normal and needed when one has been wronged. "I hate them with perfect hatred," Psalm 139 reminds us. Perfect righteous hatred does not inspire retaliation, nor does it elicit further injustice. Holy fury fuels the righteous redress of wrongs and wrongdoings. The parents of children killed by drunk drivers banded together and formed Mothers Against Drunk Driving (MADD), an organization that channels righteous rage into meaningful solutions to a real evil. At the personal level, too, hate is paradoxically a necessary (and uncomfortable) step toward forgiveness. The parent who quickly "forgives" the drunk driver without feeling outrage has probably bypassed righteous hatred. You cannot truly forgive one from whom you have insulated your true rage.

Unchecked hatred, however, can have a way of transforming itself into ugliness if it is not recognized as a step toward the ultimate goal of *healing*. As you can readily see, forgiving healing comes not from a denial of one's hurt and hatred. Nor does forgiveness erase tender scars forever stitched on the soul. A degree of forgiveness arrives only after having progressed through some very uncomfortable feelings, many of which will remain.

Eventual healing comes through being able to see the wrongdoer in a different light. By an act of sheer grace, forgiveness comes with the realization that in the complex and ambiguous decisions and mistakes we all make, the difference between wronged and wrongdoer is not as great as it feels. Reconciliation with the wrongdoer may or may not be part of the healing process. Perhaps the wrongdoer doesn't even concede guilt. Yet healing may come only to the one who realizes a degree of mutuality with the one who does harm.

Forgiveness thus conceived is quite different from our normal efforts at practicing it. True forgiveness is that which recognizes our common humanity within the confounding maze. In the words of therapist John Patton, "To be human is to recognize we are neither better nor worse than those who have injured us. We are like them. The message of the gospel is that we do not need to claim power of specialness in order to be loved and valued in God's world . . . Human forgiveness is the discovery that I am more like than unlike those who have hurt me. I am able to forgive when I realize that I am in no position to forgive."[11]

This is the point of Jesus' best known display of the meaning of forgiveness:

> [They] brought a woman who had been caught in adultery, and placing her in the midst they said to him, "Teacher, this woman has been caught in the act of adultery. Now in the law Moses commanded us to stone such. What do you say about her?" This they said to test him, that they might have some charge to bring against him. Jesus bent down and wrote with his finger on the ground. And as they continued to ask him, he stood and said to them, "Let him who is without sin among you be the first to throw a stone at her." . . . But when they heard it they went away, one by one, beginning with the eldest, and Jesus was left standing alone with the woman standing before him. Jesus looked up and said to her, "Woman, where are they? Has no one

condemned you?'' She said, ''No one, Lord.'' And
Jesus said, ''Neither do I condemn you; go and do
not sin again.''

John 8:3–11

It may not seem entirely accurate to say the bawdy
crowd had ''forgiven'' the adultress. Jesus did not ad-
monish the mob, ''Please, you are all fine upstanding
leaders of this community. Try to find it in your hearts
to pardon her. We all know she's —well—a *whore*. But
let's show her what good sports we are by dismissing her
with our 'forgiveness.' '' Jesus asked them to forgive her
not by an act of will but by an act of recognition. ''Let
him who is without sin among you . . .'' is a question
asking them not to look at *her* sin. His question challenged them to consider their commonality with her. It
was in their realization they were in no position to forgive
that she was forgiven.

Psychological and sociological and anthropological
studies and progress have not banished the social conditions that create prostitutes, drug abusers, drunk drivers, the dispossessed, or the other social ''misfits'' who
may occasionally harm us. (Neither should we blame all
crime and damage on the shiftless and homeless. You
have probably been done more real harm in your life by
gentlemen wearing three-piece tailored suits than by anyone from the ''wrong side of the tracks.'') But through
modern academic study and the social sciences we have
become more cognizant of how the conditions which
promote certain social evils are of our own creation. Even
in light of these revelations, some people in the face of
the seamy side may utter the shopworn phrase, ''But for
the grace of God, there go I,'' but they do not mean it.

What they mean is, "By the grace of God I am glad I am not like *that* lazy scoundrel." "But for the grace of God . . ." used this way is the opposite of Jesus' "Let him who is without sin . . ."

"But for the grace of God . . ." can be highly meaningful when we understand forgiveness as the recognition of our own mutual dependence upon God's grace with those in the "gutter." This forgiving grace comes as compassion upon those who, by no fault of their own, have failed, those who are so enraged by their failure, doubts, and confusion that they sometimes lash out at the world that seems to them very inhospitable, which indeed it is to them. This grace comes with the recognition that perhaps the wealth of some accentuates the poverty of others, or that the criminal justice system we have created and tolerate tends to punish less harshly those who can afford better legal representation, or that our hoarding and wasting of resources contributes to Third World unrest, poverty, and hunger. We all participate, either actively or passively, in creating and sustaining the very social conditions we most deplore. None can ultimately throw many stones.

And neither can we throw stones at the friends, family, and associates we love most, even though at times they are the ones who hurt us most. Hearts are easier to injure and be injured by those closest to striking distance! When we share private vulnerable secrets we always risk hearing them used against us in a rash temper tantrum. But the freedom of humbly sharing foibles and forgiveness with loved ones is truly one of the most a-mazing of graces. In the final analysis, to be part of a family—the "nuclear" family, a family of friends, or the family of the church—means to admit our common humanity and our sharing of life's mazes together. We do not understand completely, but in our commonness we can forgive one another's ignorance and frustration.

FRIENDSHIP AND HOPE

Elie Wiesel's wisdom will continue to serve as our guide in the other aspect of a-mazing grace at which we want to look. In one of his marvelous books of Jewish Hasidic legends, Wiesel tells of a young man who came to visit the famous Rabbi Pinhas of Koretz. The confused young man cried out:

> Help me, Master . . . I need your advice, I need your support. My distress is unbearable; make it disappear. The world around me, the world inside me, are filled with turmoil and sadness. Men are not human, life is not sacred. Words are empty—empty of truth, empty of faith. So strong are my doubts that I no longer know who I am—nor do I care to know . . . . I am unable even to study. So shaky are my foundations, so all-pervasive my uncertainties, that my mind finds no anchor, no safety. It wanders and wanders, and leaves me behind. I open the Talmud and contemplate it endlessly, aimlessly . . . I cannot go farther . . .

Who could better describe the feeling of the labryinth, the aimlessness and turmoil of attempting to answer the riddles of emptiness and uncertainty?

But the story continues. The sage Pinhas replied:

> You must know, my friend, that what is happening to you also happened to me. When I was your age

I stumbled over the same obstacles. I, too, was filled with questions and doubts . . . I was struggling with so many dark forces that I could not advance; I was wallowing in doubt, locked in despair. I tried study, prayer, meditation. In vain . . . My doubts remained doubts. I simply could not go on. Then one day I learned Rabbi Israel Baal Shem Tov would be coming to our town . . . He turned and saw me . . . The intensity of his gaze overwhelmed me, and I felt less alone. And strangely I was able to go home and open the Talmud, and plunge into my studies once more. You see . . . the questions remained questions. But I was able to go on. . . .

Wiesel closes with two of the lessons this story teaches: "God is everywhere, even in pain, even in the search for faith." And finally, "A good story in Hasidism is not about miracles, but about friendship and hope—the greatest miracles of all."[12]

Who has not ever felt doubts like those of the young man, flustered and unable to continue with daily chores? But when we share this dysfunction with a friend and discover she or he, too, has felt the same confusion, a mysterious (and miraculous) realization surfaces: I am not alone in my suffering, someone else knows and understands, I *can* go on! Hope and friendship renew us.

The miracles of friendship and hope are two consoling companions in the uncomfortable labyrinth. They are curiously fragile miracles. These two are not spectacular Steven Spielberg productions with intricate "special effects" to produce reality-distorting illusions. They are not miracles that happen apart from the normal laws of nature or scientific principles. Friendship and hope are miraculous gifts that are given simply to enable us to continue on our journey. They may provide neither clarity nor precision. But in friendship and hope we find healing. "The questions remained questions . . . but I was able to go on. . . ."

The Apostle Paul understood this when he wrote in that sublime chapter to the bickering Corinthians: "When I was a child, my speech, my outlook, and my thoughts were all childish. When I grew up, I had finished with childish things. Now we see only puzzling reflections in a mirror, but then we shall see face to face. My knowledge now is partial, then it will be whole, like God's knowledge of me. In a word, there are three things that last forever: faith, hope, and love . . ." (I Cor. 13:11–13, NEB). Paul says that in this life the mature Christian will see only "puzzling reflections in the mirror" (or in the more familiar RSV, "For now we see in a mirror dimly . . . ") But faith, hope, and love transcend the befuddlement by their very immersion in the enigmatic riddles. It is by these "spiritual gifts" within the dimness that we abide. With love, there is no bewilderment loyal friendship cannot face. With hope, there is no limit or pain that cannot be endured. With forgiveness, there is no harm that cannot find some consolation, healing, or outlet for its rage. These are the secret graces found when traversing in the maze, miracles that happen every day.

Presence And Absence In The Shadow Of The Cross

The chief sign by which Christians may know God's grace is present in the maze is the symbol of the cross. It is the symbol of suffering and redemption, Presence amid pain. As Paul wrote to the church in Philippi, in what is thought to be among the earliest "hymns" of the church:

> Look to each other's interests and not merely to your own. Let your bearing towards one another arise out of your life in Christ Jesus. For the divine nature was his from the first; yet he did not think to snatch at equality with God, but made himself nothing, assuming the nature of a slave. Bearing the human likeness, revealed in human shape, he humbled himself, and in obedience accepted even death—death on a cross.
>
> Philippians 2:4–9 (NEB)

Jesus himself made clear what following his example means: "I was hungry and you gave me food, I was thirsty and you gave me drink, I was a stranger and you welcomed me, I was naked and you clothed me, I was sick and you visited me, I was in prison and you came to me . . . Truly I say to you, as you did it to one of the least of my brethren, you did it to me" (Matt. 25:35–40).

These scriptures (and many more: see Luke 14:12–24, Luke 22:26–27, Matt. 5:3–10, Matt. 25:31–46, Rom. 6:15–23) tell us something very significant about who we are to be as Christians, even amid our confusion. These verses virtually overturn our way of perceiving the world. They inform us that God's attention is not on those above us, but on those below us. God appears not as a corporate president who must end life in cardiac care from having made too many heartless decisions; God lives in our world among those considered undesirable, those with broken hearts. Where there is oppression, rejection, pain, and confusion—there God is. For when God came to explain faith, hope, and love, we were shown a servant who suffered, one who was rejected by the "religious" leaders and ridiculed for spending time with the dregs of society. By participating in the wounds of this servant we, too, find ourselves wounded at such exposure to our own profound sinfulness as well as the opportunity for redemption.

God's very nature is to be wounded with us. And the suffering nature of God as revealed in Christ points us to an essential fellowship—the church. For it is in the context of community, what Christians recognize as the church, that we learn the meaning of a-mazing grace. In that grace, we may comfort one another within our uncomfortableness.

A moving story is told about a woman from a church in Oklahoma who, together with a team of medical personnel from across the United States, went on a mission to Ecuador. They established a small eye clinic in a shabby wooden shack high in the mountains. They dispensed glasses, performed minor surgeries, and conducted all sorts of ophthalmological procedures in less than two weeks. In this short time they treated over eleven thousand Ecuadorans! Word of the available medical help had spread quickly and so the villagers flocked to the clinic.

When it was time for the team to return to the United States, the woman from Oklahoma was given the responsibility of telling those outside the clinic that the medical team would soon be leaving and that they were sorry they would not be able to take care of everyone's needs. Almost a thousand poor people had camped outside the clinic for several days and nights in order to be treated.

When the waiting villagers saw the team packing up its supplies onto a truck, the crowd began to panic. They swarmed the clinic and began pounding on the walls and pressing through the doorway, desperately trying to receive help. The woman stood at the door and tried to shout over the mounting furor, telling them how sorry they were to be leaving. But the crowd kept pressing, shoving, clamoring for help.

Exasperated with the chaos and futility of the situation, the woman could do nothing more. They had tried to help, but it simply wasn't enough. In despair she fell to her knees and began to cry.

Then something graceful took place. A few of the peasants at the front of the throng noticed that she was weeping. They began to call out over the noise of the crowd, "She's crying, she's crying!" Shortly the shouts diminished into whispers as word swiftly passed through the crowd. A profound hush suddenly came over this once unruly mob. Some of the anguished Ecuadorans began to weep, too, while several others gently reached down to the sobbing woman, touched her cheeks with affection, and dried her tears.

In this one amazing moment, the woman said never before or since has she experienced anything quite so *desperate* on the one hand, yet so profoundly *beautiful* on the other.[13]

This is what it means to experience a-mazing grace. In fact, this is what it means to be a Christian: to find yourself in the bondage of situations that are both desperate and beautiful. If you do not find yourself in such circumstances, even only occasionally, surely you are seldom wounded and crying—but neither do you know what it means to find healing, forgiveness, friendship, or hope.

This is not a polished "happily ever after" ending. The medical team departed leaving desperately ill people behind untreated. They had not even attempted to address the complex geopolitical, economic, and cultural conditions that ignore and exploit impoverished mountain villagers needing basic medical care. But *something* compelled the medical team to try and bring healing. There was *something* that allowed seemingly hopeless peasants to comfort one who came to relieve their pain but failed. There was *something* that helped a well-meaning woman find consolation in her turmoil far from home. Even in the futility of some tattered peasants drying a woman's tears, there was *someone* who dared to whisper into the absence and void, "There is God . . . There *I am* . . ."

Somehow there was grace—consolation amid the discomfort.

Reinhold Niebuhr's eloquent words echo Paul's great "love chapter" and all we have discussed:

The final wisdom of life requires, not the annulment of incongruity but the achievement of serenity within and above it. Nothing that is worth doing can be achieved in our lifetime; therefore we must be saved by hope. Nothing which is true or beautiful or good makes complete sense in any immediate context of history; therefore we must be saved by faith. Nothing we do, however virtuous, can be accomplished alone; therefore we are saved by love. No virtuous act is quite as virtuous from the standpoint of our friend or foe as it is from our standpoint. Therefore we must be saved by the final form of love which is forgiveness.[14]

CHAPTER IV

Afflicting the Comfortable—"Grace That Confronts"

"May God deny you peace, but give you glory." [1]
—Miguel de Unamuno y Jugo

Miguel de Unamuno lived during an anguished period of his native Spain's history. Born in the Basque province of Biscay in 1864, Unamuno became a professor of Greek at the University of Salamanca. In 1914 he was forced to relinquish his position because he supported the Allies in World War I. Ten years later he was exiled because of his vehement opposition to the dictatorship of Miguel Primo de Rivera. From exile at Fuerteventura in the Canary Islands he managed to escape by boat to France, eventually making his way to Paris. He refused to return home when pardoned a short time later, even though his family remained in Spain.

By 1930 Primo de Rivera had died, and after Unamuno returned home his nation vacillated between monarchical, republican, and dictatorial forms of government. The unvanquished Unamuno hoped a "republican" solution would resolve Spain's dilemma, and for a time he believed it would—but his peace was short-lived. He almost immediately found the new "Spanish Republic" lacking. In agony he watched as his country was ultimately thrown into civil war in July of 1936. By December of that year Unamuno was dead of a "heart ailment," though his friends wondered if it was not death by a broken heart at seeing his beloved nation sundered by violence and death.

To the Spanish-speaking world Unamuno is best known as a great novelist. But to the rest he is remembered chiefly for two powerful books about faith in the modern world, *The Agony of Christianity* and *The Tragic Sense of Life*. In both works Unamuno argued that Christian faith and institutions can no longer languish in a make-believe realm of security and comfort while the dark forces of life engulf humanity in ignorance and violence. Only by embracing "agony" and the "tragic" sense of faith can Christianity demonstrate fealty to its mission. In this way Unamuno stands shoulder-to-shoulder with a long line of devotional writers who were willing to face a churning, darker side of faith (such as his fellow Spaniards St. John of the Cross and Teresa of Avila, as well as others like Martin Luther and Danish theologian Søren Kierkegaard).

Unamuno was obviously not one who stood by on the curb, casually observing the parade of events marching past his safe vantage point. Neither did he believe faith and God's grace were missing from the doubt, incertitude, and pain of his own personal agony, nor the anguished struggle of his nation. Yet Unamuno affirmed there was a relevance to faith that transcended mere comfort or assurance. In the midst of his own life in an extremely puzzling maze of personal, political, and professional turmoil, he became convinced there was a *demanding* element to grace, a radical imperative beyond the search for understanding and belief. There was to him a genuine role for grace that *forces* the faithful pilgrim toward greater openness, which yields not comfort but *dis*-comfort.

Unamuno believed there were too many people all too willing to accept God's comfort—but only precious few who were willing to take on the challenges Christians must face in a world of turmoil. In this spirit Unamuno closed his book, *The Tragic Sense of Life*, with the unsettling benediction, "And may God deny you peace, but give you glory. Salamanca, In the year of grace, 1912."

Like the searing Coventry consecration prayer, these words, "may God *deny* you peace," tumble harshly upon the ears of those who think of themselves as faithful people. Both sayings seem to cross the fine line between benediction and malediction. But to those who have been provoked by life's vicissitudes to experience discomforting grace, "grace and peace" take on a much different relationship to each other.

Not Peace But a Sword

We have seen how grace surprises and comforts, how encrusted shields of protective armor against God are pierced by unexpected grace, and how comforting grace appears in the maze offering not understanding but forgiveness, friendship, and hope. All these elements of grace help us to rebuild our spiritual lives with great faith and love for God.

But grace has another more imperative element among its multifaceted dimensions. The Bible contains a splendid image for this dual-functioning grace: the *sword*. Swords are seldom used for much but ceremony anymore, but in biblical times the sword was an indispensable weapon both of defensive protection and offensive advance. Correspondingly, the symbolic double-edged sword of God's grace cuts two ways—it brings both conviction and justice, at once judgment and mercy.

Biblical metaphors of the sword abound. Jesus unsheathed this symbolic saber when he announced, "Do not think that I have come to bring peace on earth; I have not come to bring peace, but a sword" (Matt. 10:34). And a sharp blade it would be, according to Jesus, slicing neighbor from neighbor, father from son, mother from daughter. Part of the "whole armor of God" for the Ephesians was "the helmet of salvation and the sword of the Spirit" (6:17), just as in his vision, John of Patmos saw God's mouth issuing forth a "sharp two-edged sword" (Rev. 1:16), pronouncing mercy for those who endure persecution and at the same time judgment upon the oppressors. The Hebrews were admonished to respond in faith lest God's judgment prevail and they fail to find their "rest":

> For the word of God is living and active, sharper than any two-edged sword, piercing the division of the soul and spirit, of joint and marrow, and discerning the thoughts and intentions of the heart. And before him no creature is hidden, but all are open and laid bare to the eyes of him with whom we have to do. Since then we have a great high priest who has passed through the heavens, Jesus, the Son of God, let us hold fast our confession . . . Let us then with confidence draw near to the throne of grace, that we may receive mercy and find grace to help in time of need.
>
> Hebrews 4:12–14, 16

In these passages we see that grace does not merely surprise, forgive, and comfort. The sword of grace slashes sharply in another direction. Grace indeed "comforts the afflicted"; but it also "*afflicts* the comfortable." Grace *dis*-comforts, *dis*-turbs, *dis*-orients when necessary. Rather than provide cozy approval of willful wrongdoing or misplaced ease, this grace dis-eases, dis-approves, dis-arms. It does not excuse flabby faith fattened on syrupy-sweet religious diets. It cannot idly tolerate smug "self-actualization" that eschews concrete commitments and responsibilities. God's grace cannot leave unchallenged gross insensitivities to injustice, the religious "log" in our own eye that splinters our faith and actions into pious blindspots. It opposes that which stands contrary to "faith, hope, and love." This grace must absolutely condemn evil, oppression, unjust persecution.

To hear that the same grace that comforts the afflicted also afflicts the comfortable tends to shock "comfortable Christians." And too comfortable some of the "faithful" become when refusing to confront facts they would rather not face. Our deeply rooted false assumptions, prejudices, and pretensions frequently prohibit our apprehension of God's piercing judgment. In the name of "goodness," some of us seek a fake placidity of faith that believes that the lack of heated conflict is a thermometer of spiritual health. "Christians ought to be 'nice' to everybody," our comfortable Christian declares.

But the lack of righteous conflict with injustice is really an insidious cancer steadily eroding healthy faith, a disease that eventually festers into a foul, ugly parody of faith, which in the end thwarts God's purposes. Furthermore, this malady is contagious. When allowed to spread, it can infect entire nations and denominations alike.

Against this false "too comfortable" view of faith, God's graceful judgment "afflicts the comfortable" with combative words of truth. But this grace is not antagonistic merely for the sake of conflict. Neither is it merciless wrath. This grace is the loving gift of dis-comfort that challenges us to *change*. It is grace that *confronts* and captivates our jaded inadequacies and jaundiced unconscious assumptions by compelling us to *grow*, to *correct* our shortcomings. Part of the surprising nature of grace is this very fact—our blindnesses are blindsided by the graceful dissonance between the truth and our own questionable beliefs and practices!

Graceful growth must necessarily be accompanied by "growing pains." As I have discussed in my book, *No Pain, No Gain*, spiritual growth is often nothing more than the willingness to take on the uncomfortable discipline of altering our engrained habits, be they habits of the flesh or "habits of the heart." Occasionally growth means entertaining religious ideas or concepts which at first are foreign and discomforting. Because this growth process must be painful (and because pain is by definition unpleasant), we often associate the growth only with pain, while failing to connect the pain with growth and grace. It is easy to see how "growth in grace" can gain a dis-graceful reputation.

But disgrace is not merely shameful dishonor. True *dis-grace* is the final failure to take God's judgment and power seriously. *Dis*-grace is the denial of God's challenging judgment, the *un*willingness to open one's beliefs to analysis, fervent criticism, even doubt in the service of firmer faith. Dis-grace stems not from the removal of God's ever-present love; dis-grace is our stubborn refusal to engage in dialogue with God's demands for fear we might be required to accept the pain of growth and change. Disgrace's *coup de grace* is the ultimate dismissal of ourselves from God's grace when we choose only one side of God's work revealed in double-edged pairs: conviction and justice, judgment and mercy, pain and growth. In order to remain comfortable with our faith, disgrace is our refusal to consider how God's harsh judgments may condemn our life-styles.

Jesus recurrently confronted this too comfortable "flabby faith." In fact, he seems to have reserved his harshest recriminations for those who imagined themselves the most "righteous":

> Beware of practicing your piety before men in order to be seen by them . . . Thus, when you give alms, sound no trumpet before you, as the hypocrites do . . . that they may be praised by men . . . But when you give alms, do not let your left hand know what your right hand is doing . . . so that your alms may be given in secret . . . And when you pray, you must not be like the hypocrites; for they love to stand and pray . . . at the street corners, that they may be seen by men. Truly, I say to you, they have received their reward. But when you pray, go into your room and shut the door and pray, to your Father who is in secret . . .
>
> Matthew 6:5–6

Read the twenty-third chapter of Matthew. The entire section is one long diatribe against the hypocrisies of the religious leaders of Jesus' day! Jesus calls them "hypocrites," "blind men," "vipers."

> Woe to you . . . hypocrites! For you tithe mint and dill and cummin, and have neglected the weightier matters of the law, justice, mercy and faith; these you ought to have done, without neglecting the others. You blind guides, straining out a gnat and swallowing a camel!
>
> Matthew 23:23–24

Hardly the "gentle Jesus meek and mild" praised in the plush pews at The Church of the Warm Jacuzzi!

The Prophetic Tradition

Jesus' harsh but true accusation was in the tradition of the biblical prophets. The ministry of these prophets spanned roughly the century and a half between 750 and 600 B.C. It was a particularly menacing era in Israel's history. They were times that demanded strong words aimed at the hearts of the blissfully hard-hearted. Yet the blunt sayings of these prophets reveal much about the nature of afflictive grace as it was inherited and practiced by Jesus for the purpose of repentance and change.

During the reign of King Jereboam II (approximately 786–746 B.C.), Israel enjoyed a time of peace, prosperity, and expansion. Both Israel and the southern kingdom Judah had suffered for many years under the military threat of the twin powers Assyria and Syria. The previous century had witnessed alternating periods of peace and warfare between these ancient superpowers. By the reign of Jereboam, however, the war-weary military giants had

expended themselves so fully in battle that they were left
nearly impotent to defend the territory they had seized
from Israel. In this regional vacuum of powerlessness,
King Jereboam was able to restore "the border of Israel
from the entrance of Hamath as far as the Sea of the
Armbah" (2 Kings 14:25).

Israel's military victories fostered a time of unparal-
leled domestic peace and economic prosperity. Yet the
Israelites erroneously considered their military and economic windfall a sign that they merited God's special
favor. However, this rapid accumulation of wealth created ever-deepening fissures of social class distinction
between the "haves" and the "have-nots." This disparity has been illustrated in recent archaeological ex-
cavations at Tirzah (Tel el-Farah, Israel), which reveal
vast differences between large luxurious homes and
"small huddled structures" during the century our prophets lived.[2] Apparently, Israel's enormous poverty was
only surpassed by the insensitivity of the wealthy and
"comfortable."

The prophet Amos mingled judgment with his description of the practices that created such unequal distribution
of wealth:

Therefore because you trample
        upon the poor
    and take away from him exactions
        of wheat,
    you have built houses of hewn stone,
        but you shall not dwell in them;
    you have planted pleasant vineyards,
        but you shall not drink their wine.

For I know how many are your transgressions,
    and how great are your sins—
  you who afflict the righteous, who take a bribe,
    and turn aside the needy in the gate.

                                        Amos 5:1–12

So enraptured with opulence were the comfortable that
they failed to foresee the impending doom looming on
their horizon. They remained oblivious to the old super-
power enemies to the east who were initiating a steady
military rearmament program. Instead of showing grave
concern, they were very excited about the coming "Day
of the Lord." The Israelites were convinced that this day
would bring Israel only greater prosperity, more exhil-
arating victories.

At about the same time as Amos, the prophet Isaiah
in the southern kingdom of Judah announced that the
"Day of the Lord" would not engender further exalta-
tion. The great day would bring humiliation, destruction,
devastation. It was not a forecast of "leading indicators"
the chamber of commerce would relish.

Imagine a contemporary Isaiah strolling by the lavish
shops on Fifth Avenue or Beverly Hills's Rodeo Drive
(or even among the stores and shoppers at your local
shopping mall or main street) proclaiming to all passersby:

In that day the Lord will take away the finery of the
anklets, the headbands, and the crescents; the pen-
dants, the bracelets, and the scarfs; the headdresses,
the armlets, the sashes, the perfume boxes, and the
amulets; the signet rings and nose rings; the festal
robes, and the mantles, the cloaks, and the hand-

bags; the garments of gauze, the linen garments, the turbans, and the veils.

Instead of perfume there will be rottenness;
    and instead of a girdle, a rope;
        and instead of well-set hair, baldness;
    and instead of a rich robe, a girding of sackcloth,
        instead of beauty, shame.

                      Isaiah 3:18–24

Amos pronounced the following harsh words on people who had become so comfortable with their opulence that they had forgotten how their nation was founded on the promises of justice and mercy of God. Therefore, Amos was no less scathing of Israel's hollow worship rituals:

I hate, I despise your feasts,
        and I take no delight in your
        solemn assemblies.
Even though you offer me your
        burnt offerings and cereal offerings,
        I will not accept them,
and the peace offerings of your fatted beasts
        I will not look upon.
Take away from me the noise of your songs;
        to the melody of your harps I will not listen.

                      Amos 5:21–23

To those luxuriating in ease, Amos offered dis-ease: "Woe to those who are at ease in Zion!" (6:1). "Woe" comes from the Hebrew word moaned in mourning at funerals. No wonder one of my Old Testament professors frequently reminded us would-be preachers, "Nobody ever came up to Amos after church and said, 'Nice sermon!' "

But neither Amos nor Isaiah (or any other prophets) left their message devoid of hope. Amos ended his confrontational words with one of the greatest challenges in the Bible. He admonished Israel in its metaphorically arid spiritual desert:

> But let justice roll down like waters,
>   and righteousness like an
>   ever-flowing stream.
>
> Amos 5:24

And again Isaiah intertwined judgment and mercy (and the sword image) in his description of God's wish for dealings with Judah:

> Come now, let us reason together,
>   says the Lord:
> though your sins are like scarlet,
>   they shall be white as snow;
> though they are red like crimson,
>   they shall become like wool.
> If you are willing and obedient,
>   you shall eat the good of the land;
> But if you refuse and rebel,
>   you shall be devoured by the sword;
> for the mouth of the Lord has spoken.
>
> Isaiah 1:18–20

Judgment and Judgmentalism

These prophets' proclamations about God's mercy and justice are ageless, fortunately. Unfortunately, just as ancient Israel and Judah remained deaf to the cries of the weak, poor, and the dispossessed, it seems the "least of these" often fare little better in the modern world. Just as the prophets and Jesus acted as God's agents of judgment upon the "too comfortable" of their day, modern-day prophets pronounce judgments we would rather not hear or heed. In this way Christian "prophets" are not as much predictors of the future as they are truth-tellers about how the consequences of present practices impinge upon the future.[3]

Truth-telling prophets (ancient and modern) are often accused of being judgmental troublemakers. But there is a difference between God's judgment and human judgmentalism. Judgmentalism is much like the false forgiveness we discussed earlier. A judgmental attitude elevates one's own flawed and limited opinions to the level of divine certainty. Like false "forgiveness," which actually seeks to inflict vengeance through a "holier than thou" posture, judgmentalism attempts to advance one's own selfish agenda with a counterfeit stamp of approval by God. Clothed in a pious robe of false humility, one bangs God's gavel and adjudicates *oneself* morally superior to others. This incongruity between prideful presumption and feigned humility only fosters grotesque caricatures of afflictive grace—*self*-righteousness. Buffoons who thus parody true judgment render tremendous damage to Christianity, provoking comedians, novelists, screenplay writers, and the news media into a merciless and often justified mockery of "religion." Sinclair Lewis's huckster Elmer Gantry, Flip Wilson's bogus "devil made me do it" minister, the dance-hating puritanical pastor in the movie *Footloose*, and "Saturday Night Live's" prudish Church Lady are but a few examples of comedy and fiction satirizing real judgmentalism. The public becomes so inoculated by these spurious "prophets" that they gradually build up an immunized resistance to God's true judgment.

Judgmentalism must not be allowed to dull the sharp sword of God's judgment against genuine evil and comfortable wrongdoing. Of course, even our apprehension of God's true judgment is littered with pitfalls involving our own imperfect pride, partisan political preferences, and narrow denominational agendas—what the King James Version of the Bible called the "party spirit." Yet God's judgment and mercy transcend human limits and pretensions. What we know of God, the scriptures, and ourselves dictates that we *all* stand under judgment. "All have sinned and fall short of the glory of God," Paul wrote to the Romans (3:23). But this judgment is not in the mocking sense H. L. Mencken intended when he defined a Puritan as one who harbors the lurking suspicion that someone, somewhere, might be having fun. Rather, God's graceful judgment afflicts the comfortable with the concrete realization that people in many locations are oppressed, hungry, and spiritually complacent or stagnant.

Unlike perverted prophets of judgmentalism, true prophets always include themselves under divine judgment. In this way, God's grace transcends trifling personal biases; in humble accusation yoked with acceptance of personal responsibility, persons or groups do not assume they are immune from the judgment they pronounce. Instead, they propound closer approximations to truth from the perspective of one who also stands guilty, part of the community that corporately and individually stands under God's judgment.

This kind of grace becomes a continuous mechanism possessed by a *community* of people who together discern God's judgment through a never-ending cycle of study, prayer, worship, criticism, doubt, reassessment, and action. This community gracefully confronts "too comfortable" falsities while it also celebrates comfort within the maze. It is a prime function of the church to engage in this endless process of evaluation, conflict, change, and growth. Grace afflicts the comfortable in the context of a community that will continue to care for the afflicted while ever challenging its members to grow.

When we begin to delineate specific areas where God's confrontive grace "afflicts the comfortable" in the context of community, at least three overlapping spheres of involvement emerge: the personal, national (including denominational), and international.

Enlightening The Personal Dark Side

In the personal sphere, each of us must come to grips with what psychologist Carl Jung called our "dark side." Contained in this realm are all those unconscious and semiconscious facets of our lives we frankly know little about. It is astounding to learn shortly after we marry, for instance, that we practice numerous annoying habits. Our lover is usually rather proficient at enlightening these dark areas because loved ones are close enough to see our talents and faults much more clearly than anyone else. These dark-side annoyances may become the source of some major marital or familial sparking. And soon either the offender changes or the other grows comfortable with the unnerving foibles (or if left unconfronted, a mate may suffer in silence).

These same dynamics are also at work within any deepening friendship or any healthy family. In sum, we all have our faults and limitations and are confronted with them by people who love us (and sometimes people who don't care for us either). The result: *conflict* from which we may either flee and shrink, or learn and grow.

This is much like the way God's grace confronts askew aspects of our personal lives. I once knew a woman named Peggy who discovered this grace while enrolled in a course of Clinical Pastoral Education (CPE). CPE is one of the courses in which prospective ministers receive training in personal and crisis counseling by serving as hospital chaplains. Part of the training involves participation in group evaluation sessions with other class members under the guidance of a certified leader. These sessions can sometimes become combative. The pressure and constant crises of hospital chaplaincy have a tendency to tear weak seams in one's emotional, psychological, and spiritual fabric. These tears are further ripped open during evaluation by group members who are urged to be very honest with one another (sometimes brutally so). Usually, in the course of a semester or so of this intense self-evaluation under stress, the torn spiritual garment is gradually sewn back together even stronger than before, the result of having been forced into guided constructive self-criticism. In essence, CPE is learning "grace under pressure."

This was the case with Peggy. Her life's tapestry had plenty of weak seams, just like everyone's. Describing herself before the CPE experience, she admitted having been "spoiled, timid, unsure of myself, and extremely shallow. I really didn't have many close relationships with friends, or anybody for that matter. I guess it was because I didn't want anybody getting that close to me. I thought becoming a chaplain would mean I could hide my uncertainty under a white coat and clerical collar.''

Peggy's ''moment of truth'' came the day she was asked about her shift in the emergency room. A man badly injured in an automobile accident had been rushed in by ambulance. The medical staff, despite a valiant effort, was unable to save his life. A physician on duty asked her if she would accompany him into the waiting room to notify the family. As she told the story, Peggy didn't confess to the group that she had been petrified. What do *I* have to say to someone who's just lost a husband or a father? she had asked herself desperately.

''What did you say to the family?'' a woman in the CPE group asked.

''Well, Dr. Hayes was the one who told them, he just asked me to tag along. He did all the talking. Anyway, then I went back to the—''

''Wait a minute! But what did *you* say to the family?'' the inquisitor persisted.

''Well, I didn't *do* anything. I didn't think I had to.'' Peggy could now feel her face burning.

The interrogator exploded, ''They lost their father and husband and *you* couldn't even say 'I'm sorry'? Didn't you feel *any* remorse for them? Couldn't you have just put your arms around somebody and hugged them? If you can't do that for someone who's just lost a husband, don't bother coming to *my* husband's funeral.''

Peggy was now beginning to feel hurt and angry. After a long, tense silence, someone else gently asked, ''Why couldn't you do anything, Peggy?''

"I don't know . . ." she said softly, now beginning to cry and feel extremely embarrassed.

After another long pause, she summoned some courage and replied haltingly, "I guess it just reminded me of something that happened when *my* father died. I was so angry. My father had been in the hospital for a long while. He was so heavily medicated that he was sort of half-conscious most of the time. One day I had just finished talking to him a little bit and into the room walked this chaplain. He was an absolute oaf! He looked at my emaciated father lying in bed, glanced at me, shook his head, and blubbered out in a booming voice, '*No hope, huh?*'

"I was *furious* with him. Any good chaplain should know even if a patient appears to be unconscious, his hearing is the last thing to go. His voice startled my poor father, who opened his eyes to see who had made all that ruckus. The chaplain was now surprised and said something moronic like 'Oops' as he bumbled out the door. I have never been so angry in my life!"

She gulped and blew her nose. "I keep remembering that whenever I'm at the hospital. I can't forget how it made me feel. His visit should have helped, but it didn't. I keep vowing to myself that I'm *not* going to do anything so stupid while I'm a chaplain!

"In the emergency room, I just didn't know what to say. I didn't want to say something stupid so I didn't say anything."

The inquisitor who had been so hard on her now said, "You never told us your father died. That must have been difficult. How old were you?"

"Seventeen."

The discussion shifted from her emergency room blun-

der to her father's death and how she could learn from
that experience what kind of chaplain *not* to be like! The
session forced her to recognize something about herself
that had previously remained in the dark. She hadn't
consciously considered how her father's death had affected all areas of her life. She spent many weeks thinking
about that painful CPE session. At first she was angry,
feeling as though the group had ganged up on her. But
she later noticed all the group members taking their
lumps and learning from them. She was not the only one
with problems to confront. Gradually, the discomfort
prompted her to realize that unresolved hurt and grief
from her father's death had unconsciously taught her not
to trust other people. Little by little she overcame her
timidity and mistrust. She discovered she *did* have something of value to contribute, especially with people in
pain. Her own agony taught her to speak to others in the
way she wished someone had spoken to her. Slowly, her
life was being transformed. She grew more confident and
outgoing, more gracious. She had "repented," turned
around.

Months later, reflecting on that particularly difficult
session, she said, "God's grace touched me that day. It
was in many ways the hardest day of my life. But now
I'm glad they made me look at myself more deeply."

This is how God's afflictive grace can help us rebuild
our personal, spiritual lives. Confrontational grace is a
gift we seldom immediately welcome. Criticism stings.
And the pang is oftimes worsened when biting critiques
by colleagues contain venom. God's grace stings, too.
But it is not mean-spirited, even if its messengers sometimes are. For the aim of God's afflicting grace is not
judgment in order to punish. God's judgment is aimed

at correcting faults, challenging erroneous assumptions, enlivening dead spirituality, enlightening our little known "dark side," liberating us from fear and hatred.

America! God Shed His Grace on Thee

The second realm where afflictive grace overlaps personal concerns is the national (and denominational) sphere. When it comes to grace there is a special irony embedded in American thinking. On the one hand, we lustily sing Katherine Lee Bates's beloved chorus, "America, America, God shed his grace on thee!" Our nation has indeed been blessed with abundant natural resources, a vast and beautiful landscape, a rich plurality of peoples and cultural heritages, a stable form of government, grand material prosperity.

But on the other hand, our nation tends to interpret "God shed his grace on thee" as proof we are always messengers but never recipients of judgment. By making pronouncements of judgment upon the world (but not including ourselves under those judgments), we as a nation often lapse into judgmentalism: America advises South Africa to rid itself of racial prejudice while our own courts steadily erode civil rights gains; we decry foreign tariffs that inhibit the sale of American goods abroad at the same time that we maintain policies which "protect" American manufacturers from "unfair" foreign competition; our nation, in the name of democracy and liberty, has supported dictators who, through coercion and corruption, have denied basic human freedoms to their people. The irony is that in the name of justice we frequently, though unintentionally, promote injustice.

Theologian Reinhold Niebuhr wrote extensively about this peculiarly American pretension. Our nation presumes itself virtuous, innocent, wise, and powerful—a combination of traits Niebuhr contended cannot coexist without a degree of falsification. If a nation is to be truly "powerful" in the modern world, it must by necessity sacrifice some of its virtue and innocence. The virtuous posture of America ironically prohibits us from seeing the weak seams in our cloak of innocence and power. During the post–World War II/Cold War climate, Niebuhr observed that the most poignant symbol of American prestige was atomic weaponry. He wrote: "The exercise of this power requires us to hold back the threat of Europe's inundation by communism through the development of all kinds of instruments of mass destruction, including atomic weapons. Thus an 'innocent' nation finally arrives at the ironic climax of its history. It finds itself the custodian of the ultimate weapon which perfectly embodies and symbolizes the moral ambiguity of physical warfare.⁴ We thereby find ourselves in the ironic position of manufacturing bombs to maintain peace.

While we have seen how the town of Coventry was devastated by an air raid, Niebuhr would want us to recall two other cities bombed during the war: Hiroshima and Nagasaki. The United States often forgets it is the only nation in history that has actually used an atomic weapon in hostility. Facts like this, would, according to Niebuhr, fuel the ironic incongruity between our purported virtuous innocence and the real brutality with which we as a nation wield power.

The failure to recognize this incongruity is part of our national "dark side." Our lack of awareness renders us unable to understand why many nations now look upon the United States with disdain. From their point of view, the United States used a nuclear device once, why not again? Without this crucial self-knowledge, dangerous despair may result when we engage in international negotiations. For in dealing with other nations without adequate acknowledgment of our own pretensions, the malice and distrust we encounter may drive us toward confusion or dangerous hatred or mutual misunderstandings with the "enemy." Wrote Niebuhr:

> If, on the other hand, a religious sense of an ultimate judgment upon our individual and collective actions should create an awareness of our own pretensions of wisdom, virtue, or power which have helped to fashion the ironic incongruity, the irony would tend to dissolve into the experience of contrition and an abatement of the pretensions which caused the irony. The alternative between contrition on the one hand and fury and hatred on the other hand faces nations as well as individuals. It is, in fact, the primary spiritual alternative of human existence.[5]

Niebuhr was too savvy to advocate that the "Christian" United States should unilaterally disarm. Rather, he believed the only way to lessen global tensions and to dissolve the ironic incongruity was to become aware of it and to become *contrite*. In other words, when confronted by the inconsistencies of our own national "dark side," we must not only recognize our errors but also *repent*, turn from them. This is just as true with unjust domestic politics as it is with foreign affairs. In this light, "God shed his grace on thee" is turned upside down. Much like the presumptions of Israel and Judah denounced by Amos and Isaiah, modern-day prophets like Niebuhr reveal our own pretentiousness disguised as virtue.

Amidst our comfortable accommodation to injustices come several disquieting truths: The abundance many of us enjoy is often at the expense of others. And the victims of this poverty are mostly women and their children. Of course, there is a complex sociological and economic web of causes which seem to perpetuate this spiraling decline. Yet the poor and hungry and homeless cannot afford the incongruity of rhetorical "opportunity" and "incentive" which purports to help them by cutting away their means of escape from poverty.

For us to sing "God shed his grace on thee" does not mean simply counting our many blessings; it means patriotically grappling with the tough, costly, painful, messy remedies to the social conditions that create and perpetuate injustices, inequities, and inhumanity within our own borders.

Neither are religious denominations immune from ironic incongruity or the grace that confronts them. Liberal Southern Baptists bash conservative Southern Baptists, while Methodists attempt to disgrace other Wesleyans over who is more faithful to Wesley's doctrine of grace. Meanwhile, Pentecostals tongue-lash Fundamentalists. Denominations committed to "peace and love" violently debate one another over doctrinal obscurities.

Carlo Carretto, a contemplative theologian, has meaningfully captured our dilemma of grace and the church:

How baffling you are, oh Church, and yet how I love you!

How you have made me suffer, and yet how much I owe you!

I should like to see you destroyed, and yet I need your presence.

You have given me so much scandal and yet you have made me to understand sanctity.

I have seen nothing in the world more devoted to obscurity, more compromised, more false, and I have touched nothing more pure, more generous, more beautiful. How often I have wanted to shut the doors of my soul in your face, and how I often have prayed to die in the safety of your arms.

No, I cannot free myself from you, because I am you, though not completely.[6]

God's grace afflicts those in "the comfortable pew," but not by pointing the accusatory finger at someone else. The church is us—you and me. Our nation's congregations cannot afford to split over the color of paint in the nursery while ignoring the cries of hungry babies down the street. Grace confronts and judges such silly faithlessness.

One can almost hear an Amos or Isaiah pleading, with an intent quite different than we usually presume, "America, America, God shed his grace on thee . . ."

Grace In The Global Village

The final sphere of affliction, which overlaps all the rest, is our international involvement with grace. No longer can we assume we are isolated from other nations of our world. We eat kiwi from New Zealand, bananas from Guatemala, French sorbet, drink coffee picked by the fictitiously happy "Juan Valdez" of Colombia, all while we watch Japanese televisions carrying advertisements for cars from Germany, Korea, Italy, and England.

My father-in-law recently went on a mission excursion several days journey into the jungle of West African Sierra Leone—and saw there, hung on the wall of a dilapidated village school, a picture of the space shuttle Challenger! We truly are a "global village."

This crisscrossing and converging connectedness of nations and peoples makes it increasingly more troublesome to ignore the cries of our fellow global villagers. Our neighbors seeking adequate food and water, basic human dignities of privacy and safe work clamor for freedom from oppressive government. In 1987, for example, nearly eight hundred South African coal and gold miners were killed on the job. Black miners there earn between seventy-five and eighty-five dollars per month, while their Caucasian counterparts are paid three times as much. (Since most of the gold mined is used for jewelry, these miners labor in such poverty and danger so that we may have the privilege of wearing golden crosses to church!) In this setting, where many more indignities exist, Anglican Archbishop Desmond Tutu stands as a modern-day prophet, challenging his nation and our world to stop tolerating the injustices of apartheid.

Fortunately, the international scene has many prophets who confront us with God's grace applied to specific circumstances. Archbishop Tutu, Mother Teresa, arms-reduction and human rights activists like Daniel and Philip Berrigan, and many others all provide crucial channels for God's challenging grace, which afflicts the ways we look at international *structures* of dis-grace.

Brazilian theologian Leonardo Boff writes about this grace from a Latin American religious perspective, sometimes called "Liberation Theology." "When Christians take cognizance of the link between the personal and the structural levels [of society], they can no longer rest content with a conversion of the heart and personal holiness on the individual level. They realize that if they are to be graced personally, they must also fight to change the societal structure and open it up to God's grace."[7]

By confronting international structures that impede equity and freedom, liberating grace may help usher in new possibilities of redemption for people who are suffering. The "comfortable" might (and do) argue that what suffering people need is faith and personal salvation. Of course, this is true. But as the Epistle of James notes, "My brothers, what use is it for a man to say he has faith when he does nothing to show it? Can that faith save him? Suppose a brother or a sister is in rags with not enough food for the day, and one of you says, 'Good luck to you, keep yourselves warm, and have plenty to eat,' but does nothing to supply their bodily needs, what is the good of that? So with faith; if it does not lead to action, it is in itself a lifeless thing" (James 2:14–17, NEB).

Grace, faith, confrontation, and liberation are thus yoked in an inseparable cluster of challenge. "It is not that the liberation process stands over here while grace stands over there," writes Boff. "The liberating process itself, seeking to produce a human life that is more fraternal and open to God, already constitutes the presence of liberating grace in the world. God's liberating grace is incarnated in the pain-filled but liberative course of human beings."[8]

In the "agonized" spirit of Unamuno, Leonardo Boff, along with other Spanish-speaking theologians such as José Miguez Bonino and Gustavo Gutiérrez, join pastors and lay members of base communities in their nations as well as with all the worldwide network of Christians who join hands for justice. As Unamuno realized even when this century was still young, the ongoing difficulties of this slice of the Latin world—and the struggles of Christianity to remain faithful and relevant in drastically changing cultures—demonstrate that comfortable Christians everywhere in our world need to continue to learn about being both afflicted and liberated by grace.

There is too much to be done for complacency. But neither can we afford despair.

And may God deny you peace, but give you grace.

CHAPTER V

The Cost of Grace—"Grace That Is Free Yet Costly"

Happy are they who know that discipleship simply means a life which springs from grace, and that grace simply means discipleship. Happy are they who have become Christians in this sense of the word. For them the word of grace has proved a fount of mercy.[1]

—Dietrich Bonhoeffer

Not long ago a group of ministers was having lunch together. As had been their custom lately, they entered a rather lengthy debate over a nagging concern in the church—marital infidelity among the clergy.

The discussion was particularly lively that day because a recent event had shaken their denomination like an earthquake, sending shock waves through their churches, and seriously damaging morale. A high-level denominational leader had unexpectedly resigned and hastily surrendered his ministerial credentials. (No, he was not a televangelist!) Although the official public statements about the incident were vague and evasive, rumors were rampant and everyone could "read between the lines" well enough to discern what had really happened. And yet, the fact that the whole matter remained shrouded in secrecy only aroused hostility and suspicion.

The immediate topic for the debate was the former leader's petition to be received back into the ministerial fold. He was having second thoughts not over resigning his position, but about losing his ministerial credentials.

"I don't think he deserves his credentials back!" one colleague asserted.

"But what about all the other guys who've done the same thing and have had the whole thing hushed up? We never kicked them out long enough to even talk about taking them back. I don't see that he's committed the 'Unforgivable Sin.' Why shouldn't we give him a second chance?" another asked.

"Yes. Where is forgiveness for ministers? Lord knows we all have members of our congregations who've done worse and we don't kick them out—we let them know God forgives," someone else added.

At the mention of forgiveness, one of the lunchmates suddenly protested, "Forgiveness! That would be *cheap* grace!"

"Tell me, exactly how much *does* grace cost these days? Grace isn't cheap, it's *free!*" another colleague fired back.

"Of course grace is free—but it is also *costly . . .*"

And so went the debate.

When the food finally arrived, they were so embroiled in their argument they forgot to *say* grace over the meal.

Of course, the talk of cheap grace and costly grace are echoes from Dietrich Bonhoeffer's classic, *The Cost of Discipleship*. Those familiar with Bonhoeffer know well the story of this German Lutheran pastor's imprisonment for participating in a plot to overthrow Hitler and nazism. As a pastor and theologian of the Confessing Church in Germany during that troubled time, Bonhoeffer and others like him were disturbed that the church had done so little to challenge Nazi tyranny. A long German tradition held that the church should have little to say about the affairs of the state. Part of this tradition, as old as Paul's admonition to "obey the governmental authorities," said it was one's Christian duty to follow the dictates of the rulers. Bonhoeffer had even subscribed to this view when he was younger.

Yet a change of the times wrought a change in his mind. Bonhoeffer's book, *The Cost of Discipleship* (originally titled in German, *Nachfolge*, which means simply *following*), was published in the crucial year, 1937. In the midst of the rapidly growing Nazi power, compared with a lack of activity among German churches to thwart the oppression, Bonhoeffer made his now classic distinction between cheap grace and costly grace:

Cheap grace is the grace we bestow on ourselves
. . . [It is] the preaching of forgiveness without requiring repentance, baptism without church discipline, Communion without confession . . . Cheap grace is grace without discipleship, grace without the cross, grace without Jesus Christ . . .

Costly grace is the gospel which must be *sought* again and again, the gift which must be *asked* for, the door at which a man must knock . . . Such grace is *costly* because it calls us to follow, and it is *grace* because it calls us to follow *Jesus Christ*. It is costly because it costs a man his life, and it is grace because it gives a man the only true life. It is costly because it condemns sin, and grace because it justifies the sinner. Above all, it is *costly* because it cost God the life of his Son . . . Costly grace is the Incarnation of God.[2]

For too long, argued Bonhoeffer, the church had vacillated between these polarized forms of grace; but now, in the context of Europe fraught with Fascist tyranny and poised for war, the church that had dispensed grace too easily was beginning to pay a huge price for its laxity. No longer could the church afford such a devalued version of the gospel if it was going to relate to the troubled global situation. Utilizing the idea of costly grace, Bonhoeffer's aim was to give the church a model of true discipleship in the face of such desperate circumstances:

> This message must be spoken for the sake of truth, for those among us who confess that through cheap grace they have lost the following of Christ, and further, with the following of Christ, have lost the understanding of costly grace. To put it quite simply, we must undertake this task because we are now ready to admit that we no longer stand in the path of true discipleship. We confess that, although our church is orthodox as far as her doctrine of grace is concerned, we are no longer sure we are members of a Church which follows its Lord. We must therefore attempt to recover a true understanding of the mutual relation between grace and discipleship.[3]

In other words, while the church's teaching about grace was essentially "orthodox" and correct, it sorely missed the appropriation of grace combined with the response of costly discipleship. True discipleship—the freely received yet costly response to grace—must embody the principles God demonstrated in Jesus: not mere compassion, but confrontation; not simple giving, but self-sacrifice; not easy forgiveness, but costly action on behalf of justice, truth, and morality.

With uncanny vision of the approaching holocaust, which would drastically alter the way we think of ourselves as human beings, Bonhoeffer pleaded, ''The issue can no longer be evaded. It is becoming clearer every day that the most urgent problem besetting our Church is this: How can we live the Christian life in the modern world?''—a modern world where religion and society are severed, where dictators manipulate mass communication to instill ethnic and racial hatred, where national pretensions and provincialism hasten war, and where technological advance only provides humanity with more efficient means to exterminate itself.

With an eerie mixture of prophetic pronouncement and prediction, Bonhoeffer answered his own question and penned these profound words: ''*When Christ calls a man, he bids him come and die*.''[4]

Almost exactly two years after he had been forced to leave his family and fiancée to be imprisoned, late on the evening of April 8, 1945, Bonhoeffer was suddenly moved to the Flossenburg prison. All night he was interrogated about his role in the plot to assassinate the führer. Wolf Dieter Zimmermann, the prison doctor at Flossenburg, later recalled what he witnessed the next morning:

> On the morning of the day, sometime between five and six o'clock, the prisoners . . . were led out of their cells and the verdicts read to them. Through the half-open door of a room in one of the huts I saw Pastor Bonhoeffer, still in his prison clothes, kneeling in fervent prayer to the Lord his God. The

devotion and evident conviction of being heard that
I saw in the prayer of this intensely captivating man,
moved me to the depths.[5]

As the new spring day dawned, the prisoners were ordered to strip and were led to a secluded spot. There they
were hanged.

Less than three weeks later, Hitler had committed
suicide and the Flossenberg prison was liberated.

Bonhoeffer's discipleship *had* cost him his life. And
from the witness of his life and death, God's grace took
on a profoundly visible expression in our own time. Faithful Christians will—*must*—forever honor his memory
and cherish his writings along with the host of other
martyrs who have boldly dared to speak the truth in such
dire, life-threatening circumstances.

Bonhoeffer's Legacy

Bonhoeffer's ethical diagnoses and terminology
(which found expression in several other tremendously
powerful books), validated by his witness and fate, has
immensely affected postwar Christian thinking on discipleship. Our century's wars, depressions, and oppres-
sions have ushered in a modernity that holds little space
for a wholly positive outlook on human destiny without
significant cost. In the wake of devastating destruction
and perduring injustice all over the globe, Bonhoeffer
correctly understood that simplistic versions of the Gospel offering instant "forgiveness" without true contrition, restitution, and change indeed cheapens the kind of
sacrificial love demonstrated on the cross.

It has been said that what is new about the Gospel is

not its essential message, but those who surface in each generation to give that message a new expression in their own time, space, and place. In this spirit, Bonhoeffer recognized and exemplified, perhaps better than anyone else in his generation, that there were no cheap remedies for the world's economic, social, political, or spiritual illnesses. Since the days of Bonhoeffer, many others have taken up his mantle to inform us that there are still no cheap solutions for our generation's trouble spots such as South Africa, Central America, India, Afghanistan, and many parts of the Third World. As I noted earlier, persons such as Archbishop Desmond Tutu and Mother Teresa demonstrate that discipleship in our world is, and must be, as costly as ever.

And neither has religion in the United States been insulated from many forms of cheapened grace about which Bonhoeffer spoke in prewar Germany. In fact, Bonhoeffer had studied in America and had worked in New York's Harlem district helping the poor while he was a student at Union Theological Seminary. He certainly saw as well as anyone that embedded deep within American religious history and consciousness are images of easy grace obtained by simply repeating an evangelist's magic formula for forgiveness. After this instant transformation, it may seem your primary religious duty is to cultivate good feelings about yourself that you may, in the words of the revivalist Billy Sunday's favorite hymn, "Brighten the Corner Where You Are." Too often this attitude holds little concern for issues outside our own problems. Such easy forgiveness is supposed to make us happy, wealthy, successful, and cheerful as we saw in our discussion of surprising grace. Yet this truly cheapened grace holds little room for costly discipleship, stew-

ardship, suffering, or sacrifice. Few who attend The
Church of the Warm Jacuzzi would ever consider martyrdom!

There is no doubt that in the midst of our human frailty,
which tends to repel sacrifice and eschew long-term commitments, Bonhoeffer's distinction between cheap and
costly grace helps clarify and pronounce judgment on
American Christians as well as it does any of the spiritual
problems of any place around the world or at any time
in the past.

The Cost of Pure Grace

But let's return for a moment to our lunching ministerial friends. We cannot help but wonder if they have
not corrupted the concept of ''costly grace.'' Perhaps
Bonhoeffer's words and witness have been too effective.
Maybe his intention—to forge a Christian model of costly
discipleship in the midst of diabolical evil—has, over
time and changing historical circumstance, become a bit
confused in relation to other important aspects of grace.

While certainly he wrote in a time when many had
made grace too cheap (as certainly many do in our day
as well), perhaps Bonhoeffer is now too often quoted by
those who would make grace not too cheap, but too
costly. Bonhoeffer understood that cheap and costly grace
were distinctions made within the existing Christian community of his day. But he also spoke about *pure* grace—
the unmerited, free, unconditional forgiveness God bestows upon repentant humanity. Pure grace is that which
surprises, truly encourages repentance, forgives, and provides comfort.

Bonhoeffer believed that Martin Luther understood and

experienced this "pure" grace as well as its cost. Aligning himself with a train of thought leading back to the Apostle Paul, Luther set in motion a movement of protest against those who indulged grace with monetary value. Contrary to this aberration of the power of grace, Luther, along with all the other significant reformers in both the Protestant and Roman Catholic traditions, tended to understand redemption and the forgiveness of sin by "grace through faith in Christ." Yet this "justification by faith" did not mean faith's struggle was forever completed after one's conversion. Luther had taught that after baptism one remained "*simul justus et peccator*"—at the same time "justified" (and forgiven), yet still a sinner. Even though through baptism a person could be certain of God's forgiveness, Luther also emphasized that we must struggle daily with the forces of evil to live the Christian life, the life of discipleship. To Luther the "old Adam" arises anew every morning and the "new Adam" must daily conquer sin by grace through faith in Jesus Christ.

In Bonhoeffer's mind, the problem was that Luther's followers (and by implication, other Christians as well) grasped quite well the first half of the message (saving, unconditional, unmerited grace); but they had substituted this free, pure grace for the response to that very grace, thereby cheapening the "cost of discipleship." It was the cost of our response to grace that had become too cheap. Bonhoeffer explained:

In the depth of his misery, Luther had grasp by faith the free and unconditional forgiveness of all his sins. That experience taught him that this grace had cost him his very life . . . So far from dispensing him from discipleship, this grace only made him a more earnest disciple. When he spoke of grace, Luther always implied as a corollary that it cost him his own life . . . Only so could he speak of grace. Luther had said that grace alone can save; his followers took up his doctrine and repeated it word for word. But they left out its invariable corollary, the obligation of discipleship.[6]

According to Bonhoeffer, Luther's thought had emerged to re-form both belief and response around the central principle of "justification by faith" over against the abrogations of church tradition (which had overemphasized the corollary of "good works righteousness"). Through Luther a balance was achieved between pure, unconditional, unmerited "saving" grace and what theologians call "sanctifying" grace (the grace to become holy by God-empowered acts of righteousness and goodness), which is made manifest in "costly discipleship." However, because humanity is always seeking its own interests, according to Bonhoeffer Luther's followers dropped the unsavory "costly" portion of discipleship in favor of an easier and cheaper grace. In one sense, Bonhoeffer was saying the church had overreacted to pure free grace by making the response to grace too cheap. The *response* to grace is what had become too cheap, not the initial impulse of God's gracious forgiveness.

The next step in this misinterpretation of grace, said Bonhoeffer, was when the church reduced the faith to a set of creeds for rational assent, not an experience of grace the creeds could affirm. That one should believe correctly—credal orthodoxy—become more important than having been grasped by God's grace. Modern disciples, lacking this *experience* of pure grace, had little power to manifest costly grace. They had put the "cart before the horse."

In much the same way, many in our day have confused pure, unconditional, unmerited grace with the costly response to grace. Only now, because some have benefited from and reacted to Bonhoeffer's effective challenge, some are drawn in a direction opposite to what he advocated. Having been so moved and inspired by Bonhoeffer's much needed distinction, in our admiration and devotion some of us have often made *free grace too costly while making costly grace too cheap*! Speaking on behalf of the church, Bonhoeffer was rightly concerned that when "we gave away the word and sacraments wholesale, we baptized, confirmed, and absolved a whole nation unasked and without contrition." We cheapened discipleship and its costly response to grace. The church mistakingly gave (and gives) the impression that Christian discipleship costs nothing. That is what membership in The Church of the Warm Jacuzzi means. When the church welcomes a person into its membership and makes no requirements upon her or his gifts or service or sacrifice, we cheapen God's costly grace. When congregations pander to the needs of their wealthier, more influential members as if their presence and participation (and money) were more important than that of others less socially significant, we cheapen God's costly grace. When denominations make numeric or financial growth rather than faithfulness the primary criterion for judging "success" in the church, we have cheapened God's costly grace. When our pastors become afraid to take unpopular or prophetic stands for fear of alienating "influential" people whose favor they must curry, we have cheapened God's costly grace. In short, part of our dilemma is that in making free grace too inexpensive, we have made costly grace too cheap in relation to God's self-revelation in Christ. To preach, "When Christ calls a man he bids him come die," would not prompt many members of The Church of the Warm Jacuzzi to greet the preacher after church with, "Nice sermon . . ."

On the other hand (but quite closely related), when the church cannot offer forgiveness to a repentant and broken spirit because we feel the person has sinned too grievously, we have made God's free grace too expensive. When we view God's redemption as a reward for our excellent achievement for becoming such good people rather than as the unmerited gift God's grace bestows, we have made God's free grace too expensive. When we demand a greater level of discipleship and conduct from our ministers than we do from ourselves (which is probably the reason some of our lunching ministers are so unwilling to forgive their fallen colleague), we have made God's free grace too expensive. So in making grace too expensive for others, we make free grace too costly for ourselves.

A Grace Too Expensive

As a youngster in church one Sunday morning I remember seeing an unusual sight. It still makes me feel ashamed. But this story illustrates what I mean about making free grace too expensive.

In this typical middle-class church everyone was usually neatly dressed and well coiffed, polite, and very proper. On this particular morning after Sunday school I went into the sanctuary for worship and took my accustomed spot in the balcony with my pals. From our lofty position we saw *her* enter the sanctuary and take a seat in the pews below. The woman looked horrible! Sitting among the well-kept church members, this unkempt stranger was extremely conspicuous. She had obviously been out all night doing who knows what. And worse, she was clearly from a different, more raffish "kind" than those who attended this church. Her once colorful but now faded and wrinkled party dress starkly contrasted with the staid, dark, and prim dresses of the other ladies in the congregation. Although she was pretty in a "tacky" sort of way, her fancy hairdo had become badly mussed and her bright red lipstick (anathema!) was smeared over the edges of her mouth. Tears had run the thick, black mascara under her eyes to give her the look of a raccoon. She was obviously distraught. But what deed had drawn her here to church after such a wild night?

In this gathering purporting "agape" love, with mouths agape, everyone—and I do mean everyone—stared at such a sight, at such an indignity. How dare one such as her come to church looking like that! People whispered to one another, carefully glancing askance, trying to glimpse the hussy without being distasteful or obvious.

She sat alone through the whole service, self-consciously trying to rise and sit at the proper times the rest of us knew by heart, singing the hymns while nervously aware that hundreds of eyes were upon her. She was out of place and she knew it. Church is the sanctuary for the saints, we all thought and effectively communicated nonverbally. It is a place only for those who behave correctly, only for those who never fail or waiver, for those whose common sense and morality keep

them from ever ending up like *her*. We Methodist pharisees snorted self-righteous prayers while pointing to the
lipsticked publican pounding her chest in contrition.

After the service came the usual scramble to dash home
before the pot roast burned. And no one—not *one*—
spoke to her. She awkwardly stood around for a while
as if she were waiting for something to happen, then left
with her head bowed, quietly passing others who also
lowered their heads to avoid eye contact. I remember
thinking it was too bad she didn't go out the door where
the minister always stands and greets the people who
come by to tell him he gave a nice sermon. Maybe he
would have talked to her. After all, he's supposed to do
that kind of thing.

The memory of her still haunts me. The members of
that church were not "bad" people; we were people of
religious habits—habits sometimes communicated much
more effectively than the faith we truly felt united us.
Maybe she was inspired or helped by the service, but I
doubt it. I never saw her return. Yet the church had
something special to offer her. She sensed that and she
came. But at that time we could no more offer her what
she needed than she could articulate that need. What is
ironic about this story is that both of us needed the same
thing: grace. For her, some sin, a growing disgust, or a
gnawing weariness of life-style had caused her to come
vaguely seeking the grace to be forgiven or to change.
Her act of faith by walking through the door and remaining amidst stares and whispers was proof enough of
her desire for repentance. And God's loving grace and
forgiveness and healing were as close as a friendly handshake, a smile, and some encouraging words with an
invitation to return next week for worship. Grace cannot

be learned or accepted all at once. It takes repetition, the rhythm of weekly gathering with other people who are trying to understand and then live in grace. That's one way we learn about it. But she didn't experience the repetition of worship and grace with us. I hope and pray she didn't give up and that someone else responded gracefully.

Whereas back then I remember feeling sorry for her, now my regret tends more toward those like us who cannot seem to respond to a person like "her." Under the guise of celebrating grace and faith, we demonstrated how little we knew about them. "When did we see you, or feed you, or clothe you, Lord?" Mine is not necessarily sorrow over a cruel misdeed—though cruel and a misdeed it was to refuse comfort to the Lord disguised in streaky mascara and a faded party dress. It is more like remorse that a larger number who professed to know better did not know more of free grace ourselves. For if we had, it would have been a simple matter to tell her about it, or at least to admit how much we didn't know about it. Sometimes just knowing you don't understand together makes a person feel better.

The point is this: The grace we knew was too expensive for one such as her. She did not yet need to learn of costly response; that would surely come in time. She yearned for and deserved God's *free* offer, a touch of liberating, forgiving love, a word that surprising, amazing, comforting grace could be hers if she allowed herself to be grasped by the same love of God that gives us courage to seek it in places of worship and among those who claim its power to redeem.

People like her are the *cost* of grace that is too high,

free grace made too costly for others because we make it too expensive for ourselves.

A Grace Too Cheap

A friend of mine remembers an incident from his past equally telling, only his is a tale of grace too cheap. He grew up in the South during the turbulent 1960s. Boycotts, protest marches, and demonstrations pitted racial equality against long-cherished assumptions equating the status quo with paternalistic discrimination. He recalls an April evening in 1968 when his small country church was conducting a week of revival services. Revivals were something to which my friend had become accustomed. Every year the same old evangelist would come and preach to the same old congregation about repenting by coming to the same old altar and praying the same old prayer, asking Jesus to come into their hearts and cleanse them from the same old sins of lust, envy, and gossiping. Every year everyone went to the altar. The evangelist wouldn't quit preaching until they all did!

On this particular night the air was filled with a special excitement and my friend was one of the last "holdouts" —most everyone else had been to the altar that week but him, and time was growing short. Like the hussy at the other church, he felt the pressure of a hundred pairs of eyes fixed upon him. The evangelist's pleading seemed interminable. But he had been thinking about why everyone seemed electrified on this evening above the others. It was the same day Dr. Martin Luther King, Jr., had been shot outside his motel room in Memphis. It had been an anxious and unsettling evening; they had not yet heard about the fate of Dr. King when they began their revival service.

Finally the evangelist's hoarse harangue reached its highest crescendo. My friend gave in before he knew the evangelist would stop the singing of "Just As I Am" and call him out by name, declaring the specific adolescent sins for which he thought my friend needed forgiveness. He haltingly approached the altar to supportive shouts of hallelujah and amen. But he was just going through the motions. His spirit was in Memphis. He knew how much Dr. King meant to some of his friends at school. And so he worried and wondered until, mercifully, the last amen was sung.

Afterward, everyone was lingering and chatting outside the small wooden frame church when someone who had been listening to a car radio shouted out, "King's dead! I just heard it, he's dead!" What happened next changed my friend's life and his faith.

Almost everyone around him burst into cheers upon hearing this news. It was not unlike the very same mouths in Jerusalem, centuries ago, who could triumphally shout "Hosanna" on Palm Sunday, yet cry "Crucify Him" a few days later. To some in Jerusalem, Jesus was not a liberator but a malcontent, and they were glad to be rid of this menace to their way of life. The irony did not escape my friend, though he was only a young man. In the middle of that display of hypocrisy and racism, he made his real commitment to Christ. He silently pledged to God that he was going to be a part of that which would change hypocrisies like those immediately around him that moment.

Like the members of the other church who had little to say to a "hussy," these were not "bad" people, either, though their racism was abhorrent. Rather, they, too, were in need of grace—but a grace quite different than was preached in their revivals. If the woman with the faded dress had stumbled into their church on the night of the revival, they would have known *exactly* what to do and they probably would have helped her. And perhaps their repetition of free grace would have helped her understand God's forgiveness. But their grace was not color blind. They would have responded quite differently if a black person had come pleading on behalf of basic rights which ought to belong to any human being, rights for which Christians ought to be more committed than anyone because of our belief in God's love for all people. We can hope attitudes are different now in that little church, though many would say they aren't.

At that time these people had made grace so cheap they were unable to see its racial consequences in the context of their culture and unique history. They were in need of another aspect of this grace, its cost. It is not enough to tarry at the altar of commitment and never translate the effects of that commitment into the larger realm of society. To speak of "freedom in Christ" is exceedingly hollow while oppression undergirds a posh or oppressive life-style. The response to grace must confront us with the costly recognition that all is not necessarily right with the world just because we are "right with God," that forces of societal evil hold too much power not to be taken seriously, and that the greatest evil is sometimes that which is done in the name of God or goodness.

And so in the name of what they thought to be "goodness," many could cheer the death of a King; but by their cheering they displayed a need for grace more graphically than any sin their evangelists could possibly accuse. That is the trouble with those who make grace too cheap for themselves. But the example of Christ suffering on a cross is not merely easy forgiveness, it is the very model of costly sacrifice made for those who do not appear to deserve it, but who in God's sight are immeasurably precious. Dr. King not only demonstrated this sacrificial quality in his life, he was also aware that the imperfections of the church (or of any individual, including himself) must not stop it from acting in the world on behalf of those in need of grace. Nor should hypocrisy cause abandonment of the church. In his profound *Letter from a Birmingham Jail*, while he referred to God's judgment upon the church for its lack of commitment to the causes of righteousness for the dispossessed, King also wrote, "I am thankful to God that some noble souls from the ranks of organized religion have broken loose from the paralyzing chains of conformity and joined us as active partners in the struggle for freedom." It was his very death in the contradictory context of cheering revival-goers that King made of my friend a convert who is now a minister of Jesus Christ working for justice and righteousness.

These two stories taken together well illustrate our twin dilemma with the cost of grace: a free grace too expensive and a costly grace too cheap.

The Balancing Act

With this distinction in mind, we must attempt to recover a proper balance between free and costly grace. As with all the other forms of grace we have discussed, free and costly grace are but part of *the* grace of God, expressed and described in many differing yet unified ways. And so we must affirm both tenets of free and costly grace advocated by Bonhoeffer when kept in their proper perspective and balance.

Keeping grace's cost in balance means affirming three beliefs about God's grace.

First, we believe that God's initiative of grace is free, unconditional, unmerited.

We have already seen (chapter 2) how Paul's conversion was a surprising experience of free and unmerited grace. We saw how this grace counteracts our cultural, psychological, and spiritual need to "pay our dues," releasing us from our "spiritual safes," which insulate us from grace. Other biblical accounts also help us understand this unconditional nature of God's grace. Particularly familiar are the parable of the Prodigal Son (Luke 15:11–32), the story of the paralytic lowered through the roof (Mark 2:1–12 and Luke 5:17–26), and Philip's baptism of the Ethiopian eunuch (Acts 8:26–40). When the father gladly went out to greet the prodigal who returned home after realizing his error; when Jesus saw the faith of the paralytic and his friends who lowered him through the roof to be healed; when the Ethiopian searching for spiritual truth offered himself for baptism—all these and many more passages display the same characteristic of grace: God's unconditional acceptance of a penitent person. Of course, one could argue repentance was necessary for grace. While repentance was a precondition for grace to be triggered, it did not prefigure Christ's gracious invitations. Repentance is the desire to be "turned around" by a grace always present, a willingness to cooperate with God's initiative in order to change, to head down a different path. Without this willingness, grace has little room for its surprises, as we have seen. But grace is present even if willingness is not.

Many great Christians throughout the ages have been granted this wonderful experience of unconditional grace, often after long attempts to "pay their dues." While we have lingered longer with Bonhoeffer and Luther, Paul and Augustine, another historic figure whose pilgrimage displays this central experience of grace was John Wesley, the founder of Methodism.

Wesley's religious life in early eighteenth-century England was one of devout piety. His cleric father and deeply religious mother provided disciplined education in the faith. He had attended Oxford University and, upon deciding to become a minister of the Church of England, took very seriously his preparation for ordination. He was a learned and highly disciplined man who labored so methodically that his small band of student followers at Oxford were mockingly dubbed "methodists." So zealous was Wesley that he decided to come to the American colonies and try to convert the Indians of Georgia.

But Wesley's voyage to America was a disaster. His life was fraying at the edges. Aboard the storm-tossed ship carrying him from England, Wesley was a nervous wreck. As if to rub salt in his spiritual wound, the violently swelling ocean made Wesley fearful for his life and for his eternal destiny, should the ship not withstand the storms. Wesley's seagoing passage was like Jonah's in reverse—he was willfully journeying to carry this cold, methodical gospel to the "heathen," but he was ironically in need of the warmth of grace himself! Wesley was greatly impressed, however, by a small band of

German Pietist missionaries called Moravians who were also on board ship. While stormy gales rocked the small vessel, the Moravians prayed and sang with an assurance of grace Wesley felt he badly lacked.

Wesley's attempt to convert the Native Americans was an utter disappointment and he finally returned home an abject failure. The one who had prided himself on being so religious and zealous was now searching for something he could not quite yet put his finger on. Then, on May 24, 1738, Wesley was invited to a prayer meeting. He wrote this now famous passage in his diary that night:

> In the evening, I went very unwillingly to a society in Aldersgate Street, where one was reading Luther's Preface to the Epistle to the Romans. About a quarter before nine, while he was describing the change which God works in the heart through faith in Christ, I felt my heart strangely warmed. I felt I did trust in Christ, Christ alone for my salvation; and an assurance was given me that he had taken away my sins, even mine, and saved me from the law of sin and death.[7]

This heartwarming experience changed Wesley and altered the course of the church. Most important for our purpose is that his experience, like those of Paul and Augustine, shows the power of grace to work over a long period of time in changing someone's life, even before one becomes aware of that grace. Most powerfully, such grace came as a free gift to one who so desperately tried to earn salvation but could not.

As we have already noted, our society is plagued by those trying to earn free grace. Attempting to earn grace is the chief reason we make free grace too expensive. But we cannot earn grace. It is not "earnable." Earning implies working for and deserving compensation. But hidden just beneath the attractive half-truth that we ought to earn grace is the fact that grace is already a free gift. Grace is free because it is God's nature to give freely. While most of our experiences do not have the drama or history-changing consequences of a John Wesley, a Martin Luther, or a Dietrich Bonhoeffer, free grace makes God's claim upon each of us no less than each of them. From the Gospel and the lives of a "great cloud of witnesses" in our Christian heritage, we learn that God's grace does not seek value; grace creates value.

Secondly, we believe that from God's free and unmerited initiative of grace, our *response* in grace must indeed be costly.

Often, the problem of balancing free grace and costly response is made out to be a problem of chronology. Once one experiences the free grace of God, so the argument goes, only then may one proceed to make responses by costly grace. It is easy to see why the debate takes this form. When we initially experience the grace of God, we often feel we must *do* something, though we are not always sure what is the right thing to do. Still, we all have a pretty good idea what the basic ethical injunctions are; we think of the Ten Commandments as well as thousands of rules that are best to follow. So in response to grace we *behave*. Yet as Bonhoeffer (and many others before and since) observed, sometimes in our zeal we relocate the ethical injunctions chronologically before the experience of grace and its affirmations about God. This move, if it becomes extreme, distorts God's grace by substituting expensive grace (legislating behavior) for free grace (unconditional acceptance), as illustrated by the woman who came to church and was not welcomed.

I once knew a woman who to all outward appearances was a model Christian and exemplary church member. She volunteered to help at all the church dinners and fund-raising projects. If there was any committee meeting or announced gathering at church, she would be there. Her devotion seemed inexhaustible!

But one afternoon I found her sitting alone in the church kitchen where she had been scrubbing the floor. She was physically exhausted and emotionally frazzled. "Why don't you go home," I told her, "you really don't need to work this hard around here."

"But I *have to*!" she said urgently, struggling to her feet.

"Oh, this silly floor can wait," I assured her. "In fact, why don't you just take a little vacation from church work? You've done so much around here, I think you deserve a break as much as you need one."

"No! You don't understand!" she shrieked. "I have to do all these things around here—I just *have to*!"

"Why do you have to?" I asked.

A stern look suddenly came over her tired face. She brushed a wisp of stray hair back in place and said, "If you *must* know, I did something terrible a few years ago—something so bad I've never told anyone about it. I have to do all these things to make up for it—I just *have to*."

Like most of us, she had done something of which she was ashamed. She had been around the church enough to know grace is costly. But somehow she had missed the idea that costly grace is the *response* to forgiveness, not an attempt to earn it.

In contrast to her is another woman I know. She, too, diligently volunteers for a host of activities in the church. She especially likes to help people in need. Having experienced the misplaced motivation of the lady scrubbing the floor some years before, I was wary of this other woman who seemed to spend even more time around the church. I asked her once why she did so much. I braced myself for another sad story about the confusion between free grace and its costly response.

"Some years ago I went through a divorce," she explained. "It was the most devastating experience of my life. I felt guilty and angry and lonely. I hadn't had much to do with God before that—but God and this church surrounded me with love at the time in my life when I needed it most.

"Even though that's been several years ago, I'm still grateful for all the love and support I received then. And so I like to do all I can to help other people feel that same way."

What a beautiful story about the balance of free grace and its costly response! In her there is little of the frazzled pace of the other woman scurrying to pay for grace. Rather, in response to the experience of freedom God's grace provides, she devotes her life—often in costly ways—to serving the God who healed her hurt.

It is important to notice that to outward appearances both women performed good deeds. Placed side by side, one could notice little difference. But there is a vast difference between the *inner* qualities of grace motivating each of them. While the first woman attempted to earn God's grace by mercilessly pushing herself beyond all boundaries of endurance, the second woman performed costly acts in response to God's free grace. The imbalanced view of grace by the first woman produced emotional, physical, and spiritual depletion. But the good deeds of the second woman demonstrate that when costly acts of discipleship flow forth from a steady stream of God's love and acceptance, a balance of free and costly grace may result.

Minister and writer William Willimon has observed that balancing free and costly grace is not as much a matter of chronology as it is of understanding that ethics flow out of our faith in God and our experience of God's free grace: "Christian ethics arise out of Christian faith. That is why Paul, in his letters to young churches, lists his ethical injunctions after his theological affirmations. First he talks about God, then with a transitional 'therefore' or 'because,' he talks about the implications of God's behavior for our behavior. Paul believes that our actions flow from our being."[8]

When costly ethical actions flow from our faith in God as that faith is renewed daily, then our experience of and response to grace becomes part of our day-to-day duty of discipleship. Christian discipleship, then, involves a delicate balance of acting out all of God's grace. Of course, demonstrating grace is no small task. That is why a community of faith sharing "life together" (the title of another of Bonhoeffer's books) becomes so important for support and nurture. In the context of a community of faith, we together encounter Christ and begin to fathom what it means to allow faith to flow forth in costly actions:

Acting like a Christian is not so much a matter of thinking about an appropriate path of action and then courageously deciding to do it. Christian action is more like the matter of being in love with someone. When we are in love our energies are released, our attention focused, our goals redirected, and our whole picture of the world transformed . . . We do not so much decide to be good or courageous as become attached to some object of love and attention that reinforces and releases our energies so that our good actions become, not an act of will but a response to the beloved . . . We are obedient to whatever absorbs our attention. Therefore, the church is engaged in ethical activity whenever—in worship, prayer, education, music, storytelling, social action—it focuses our attention on the beloved (Christ).[9]

Our problem in these focused loving relationships ultimately prompts the question, "How much can I commit myself?" or even "How much do I *want* to commit myself?" Despite how much "in love" we may feel, there are human limitations (real or imagined) to our capacity to act out our devotion. Yet in engaging Christ our limitations, allegiances, and responsibilities become clarified, shaped, and challenged. And in this engagement with Christ we also come to understand that free and costly grace are not chronological but dynamically interdependent parts of our entire experience of God's grace. Costly grace is that part of the whole which compels us to act upon our experience of free grace. Activity does not validate the experience of grace as much as action flows from grace.

One of the Biblical accounts illustrating this point is

that passage describing Jesus' encounter with the man by the pool of Bethzatha:

> Now there is in Jerusalem by the Sheep Gate, a pool in Hebrew called Bethzatha, which has five porticoes. In these lay a multitude of sick invalids, blind, lame, paralyzed. One man was there, who had been ill for thirty-eight years. When Jesus saw him and knew that he had been lying there a long time, he said to him, "Do you want to be healed?" The sick man answered him, "Sir, I have no one to put me into the pool when the water is troubled, and while I am going another steps down before me." Jesus said to him, "Rise, take up your pallet, and walk."
>
> John 5:1–8

A local legend about this pool attracted the ill. The legend stated that occasionally an angel came to stir or "trouble" the water in the pool (it possibly contained a mineral spring which bubbled up from time to time) and that the first infirm person to enter the troubled water would be healed. What a sorry sight this must have been with all sorts of invalids lying around waiting to make a mad dash to be the first into the water. At first glance, it may seem rather cruel that Jesus should ask this unfortunate man, "Do you want to be healed?"

But the text takes special care to emphasize the man had been there thirty-eight years. *Thirty-eight years!* A lifetime in the life expectancy of the ancients! One would think that in nearly four decades the man would either succeed or give up trying to be healed in the pool. Hence, the implication behind Jesus' question runs deeper into the man's true illness: "Do you *want* to be healed?"

We can imagine there might have been a good deal of camaraderie around that pool where the man had dwelt so long. It was a busy and interesting place, situated by one of the main entrances into Jerusalem, a major international trade center even then. A lucrative begging enterprise was likely flourishing at the gate, financial transactions between the ill, and busy but sympathetic passersby. Certainly one couldn't help but pity the plight of this motley sampler waiting for their dip into the healing waters. Yet, the lives of these sufferers quite possibly had their own comfortable charms, friendships, and consistent if modest expectations.

"I have no one to put me into the pool when the water is troubled," answered the man. It wasn't really an answer as much as an excuse from responsibility. Confronted with the possibility of leaving his familiar surroundings, of finally taking responsibility for himself after thirty-eight years of begging, of leaving his comfortable albeit lowly life to take the risk of life on the outside, the man simply made an excuse.

"Do you *want* to be healed?"

In the words of a sermon title I once read, the beggar's reply to Jesus' question might well have been, "No thanks, I'd rather be sick . . ."

But grace confronted him through this encounter when Jesus said, "Rise, and walk." To respond to the free invitation of grace also meant accepting its cost; it demanded recognition of the interdependence of free yet costly grace. Healing for him also entailed taking on responsibility for himself. And so when he arose, he was healed. It was not a matter of chronology as much as one of responsibility. (Also see the story of Bartimaeus, Mark 10:46–52, as well as Matt. 20:29–34.)

The story of the young rich man tells of another who was troubled by the cost of grace in an encounter with Christ (Matt. 19:16–22). This young man wanted to know: "Teacher, what good deed must I do, to have eternal life?" After Jesus had given him an abbreviated version of the Law, Jesus challenged him: "If you wish to go the whole way, go, sell your possessions, and give to the poor, and then you will have riches in heaven; and come, follow me" (NEB). Of course, the young man went away sorrowful, for this grace was too costly for him.

Yet there was another wealthy disciple who took to heart this relationship between free and costly grace. Zacchaeus was a dreaded and dishonest tax collector, a man "small of stature," probably the kind of teenager other kids make fun of in junior high for being too short. And what better way was there to get even than for Zacchaeus to legally "stick it to 'em" through the corrupt system of Roman tax collection? Easy to see why Zacchaeus was a wealthy outcast.

When Zacchaeus came to the parade and climbed the sycamore tree, Jesus made him a gracious but costly offer: He wanted to stay at Zacchaeus' home. While this was a gracious gesture to the hated tax collector, it was a costly one for Jesus. Jesus and Zacchaeus both understood ostracism, and Jesus' offer outraged the proper religious sensibilities of the leading citizens who had been swindled by this tax-collecting scallywag. But in this encounter intermingling free and costly grace, Zacchaeus saw the connection—if he was to be able to receive Jesus' gracious initiative, he could respond in kind to its costliness. And so he freely offered to return fourfold what he had cheated to his neighbors and gave half his possessions to charity. Jesus told him, "Today salvation has come to this house!" Free grace cost Zacchaeus all he had! But through grace and its costly response he found true discipleship as well as Bonhoeffer's "fount of mercy."

These stories about free and costly grace demonstrate the necessity that the two be held together and not confused with each other. They should be held in creative tension, a value we learned with a-mazing grace.

A third point about balancing free and costly grace should close our discussion. As I indicated in the preface, we believe that all kinds of grace—including costly and free, along with a-mazing, comforting, confronting, sacramental, or whatever form of grace we would wish to identify—are all only glimpses of the entire unity of God's gracious gift of love. It is one gift, one grace, manifested differently and only clumsily described.

For Christians, the model and symbol of this grace of God is the cross of Christ. When viewed like a prism, differing angles of vision refract various colors among the rainbowlike spectrum of God's gracious activity. Too often, the meaning of the cross is constricted within forgiveness for sin alone, a view that represents a portion of the truth, yet misses other significant aspects of grace. For in the cross we see God's surprising grace through the paradoxical relationship between weakness and true strength. To a world that understands strength only in terms of success and power, the cross exemplifies power found in apparent weakness, the paradox that "God chose what is foolish in the world to shame the wise, God chose what is weak in the world to shame the strong, God chose what is low and despised in the world, even things that are not, to bring to nothing the things that are, so that no human being might boast in the presence of God" (I Cor. 1:27–29). Moreover, in the cross we see God's presence revealed in a-mazing suffering, a fact that confronts us with the cost of grace. For in this terrifying cross and its aftermath come both the symbol of our dilemma and the power to act: God has freely given, at great human cost, an expression of love that communicates unconditional grace to the most undeserving ("Father, forgive them; for they know not what they do"—Luke 23:34), while at once challenging the redeemed to acts of discipleship.

Jesus' postresurrection appearance to Peter in John 21:15–25 demonstrates this challenge of discipleship. This story shows how costly discipleship must flow forth from faith in the free grace of Christ, the grace already demonstrated on the cross. Jesus, you recall, repeatedly questioned Peter, "Do you love me?" The passage contains an interesting wordplay not easily translated into English. Jesus' word for "love" is the Greek *agape*— the unconditional, self-giving, and sacrificial love used to describe God's love. Yet in his affirmation and response, "Yes Lord, you know that I love you," Peter used another Greek word for love, *philia*—the somewhat lesser "filial" or "brotherly and sisterly" sort of affection. Peter's response reveals a certain shallowness of faith, or in our terms, a cheapened grace. To this "cheapened" response immediately follows the costly command, "Then feed my sheep." Peter was being instructed to substantiate his love of Christ with acts of true discipleship.

I John 4:19–21 continues to express this lesson most clearly: "If anyone says, 'I love God,' and hates his brother, he is a liar; for he who does not love his brother whom he has seen, cannot love God whom he has not seen. And this command we have from him, that he who loves God should love his brother also.'' The reciprocal relationship between free and costly grace, drawing sustenance from Christ's crucifixion and resurrection, challenges us to express our faith in costly discipleship.

Examples of grace in Christ cited in nearly two millennia of Christian thinking, believing, and writing have not yet exhausted the discovery of how Christ's life, death, and resurrection symbolize the mystery of the unity of grace, of loving Christ and loving the neighbor, the delicate balance between free and costly grace. Absolute balance is never truly reached. Because we are all limited in our understanding and actions, we need the community of faith to challenge our imbalanced views on grace. In the mysterious ''body of Christ''—the community of faith of which we are a part—our weaknesses are challenged by others' strengths, just as our strengths in turn challenge the shortsightedness of others. Such is the mystery of acting out God's grace. While it isn't terribly satisfying to say this unity of grace is a mystery, it seems when we try to comprehend and describe our experiences of grace that we are only nibbling on the edges of the limits of our language. We have a yearning, a churning desire to know and to clarify, identify, and classify grace as if it were a drop of pond water under a microscope. Yet attempts to scientifically analyze grace must ultimately end in failure. For talking about grace takes us to the very limit of our powers of definition and description, oftentimes bringing torrents of confusion. Yet like the towering Coventry Cathedral, the cross stands above the rubble of centuries as the central symbol of Christian self-understanding and history, a signpost amid both hurt and joy that grace comes in many mysterious forms. It is free and amazing, costly and afflictive.

Even in our confusion we may be comforted by the writers of Scripture. For at times they, too, admitted a lack of understanding, which itself was a cause to "grow in grace":

Therefore, beloved, since you wait for these, be zealous to be found by him without spot or blemish, and at peace. And count the forbearance of our Lord as salvation. So our beloved brother Paul wrote to you according to the wisdom given him, speaking as he does in all his letters. There are some things in them hard to understand, which the ignorant and unstable twist to their own destruction, as they do the other scriptures. You therefore, beware lest you be carried away . . . and lose your stability. But grow in grace and knowledge of our Lord Jesus Christ. To him be the glory both now and to the day of eternity.

                                    2 Peter 3:14–18

CHAPTER VI

Aweful Grace— "Life Itself Is Grace"

Listen to your life. See it for the fathomless mystery that it is. In the boredom and pain of it no less than in the excitement and gladness: touch, taste, smell your way to the holy and hidden heart of it because in the last analysis all moments are key moments, and life itself is grace.[1]

—Frederick Buechner

Miracles are nothing other than God's ordinary truth seen with surprised eyes.[2]

—Gerald G. May, M.D.

Not long ago, while we were visiting family on the Olympic Peninsula of Washington State, one clear evening we climbed a mountain peak in the national park to watch the sunset. The commanding view from atop Hurricane Ridge was probably the most majestic sight I've ever seen.

From the mountaintop, to the northwest, was a breathtaking view of the Strait of Juan de Fuca separating Washington from Canada. A mysterious silvery fog had just begun creeping across the water. Directly below us golden sunlight danced on rippled water beyond the little logging town of Port Angeles, its city lights glimmering in the twilight. And to the south and east and southwest nothing was visible but the snowcapped grandeur of Mounts Carrie and Olympus and countless other surrounding peaks and valleys. Each moment the setting sun cast an explosion of colors, which coated the alpine ranges with ever-changing hues of reds, yellows, azure, and purple. These colorful splashes contrasted vividly with mountains edged in white snow and the dark greenery of hemlock, spruce, cedar, and Douglas fir. Meanwhile, wild deer nibbled the grasses on the hillside only a few feet away. Every breath of chilled evening air was charged with the solemn energy of the moment.

The whirling 360-degree panorama was one of those experiences both delightful and sacred—a thrill I hope to repeat in the future—religiously!

We have all had this kind of ''mountaintop'' experience, at least I hope you have. They are moments when, trapped in the valleys between urban mountains of concrete, chained to washer-dryer combinations, or cramped into makeshift office cubicles, we are permitted to emerge long enough to reconnect ''nature and nature's God.''

Creation And Redemption

In such utterly speechless moments, the mysterious quality of grace overpowers us. It occurs in a stealthy sort of way; it is as if for a little while we have been suddenly overwhelmed by someone or something so beautiful and timeless that we are momentarily transfixed in wonder. The moments need not be only encounters with nature; they may be intimate feelings of warmth found in relationships with others, inspirational moments in worship, a spine-tingling orchestral crescendo, any time when *awe* strikes. And when the wonder sinks in, we realize it was a precious gift interjected into creation, a redemptive moment of grace.

The prologue to the Gospel of John links creation and redemption in this mysterious way. Echoing Genesis 1:1,

John's Gospel begins: "In the beginning was the Word, and the Word was with God, and the Word was God. He was in the beginning with God; all things were made through him, and without him was not anything made that was made" (John 1:1–3). Likewise, Psalm 33 poetically connects God's acts of creation and redemption:

> For the word of the Lord is upright;
>> and all his work is done in
>>> faithfulness.
> He loves righteousness and justice,
>> the earth is full of the steadfast
>>> love of the Lord.
>
> By the word of the Lord the
>> heavens were made,
>> and all their host by the breath
>>> of his mouth.
> He gathered the waters of the sea
>> as in a bottle;
>> he put the deeps in storehouses.
>
> Let all the earth fear the Lord,
>> let all the inhabitants of the
>> world stand in awe of him!
> For he spoke, and it came to be;
>> he commanded, and it stood forth.
>>>>> Psalm 33:4–9

While we have seen how grace surprises, comforts, confronts, and costs, this graceful linking of creation and redemption inspires and nurtures us. It brings the deepest realization that "mountaintop" moments are sacred pauses in the numbing march of time; and in their blessed mysteriousness, these moments are sacramental—they are *aweful*.

Awe And Grace

The word *awful* has unfortunately acquired a rather bad reputation. Popular verbiage has reduced it to the "very bad, the very ugly." Even worse was the popular California "Valley Girl" cliché *awesome*, which has been used vaguely to praise anything from a bronze suntan or a tasty taco to an exciting surfboard ride. But the terms *awesome* and *awful* need to reclaim their spiritual roots. While *awful* as defined in *Webster's Dictionary* can indeed mean "extremely bad or unpleasant" as well as that which is "impressive," it also may describe "that which inspires awe . . ." In turn, *awe* is defined as "Fear mingled with admiration or reverence; a feeling produced by something majestic, sublime . . ." These definitions make it clear we ought to distinguish between *awful* (meaning bad) and—if I may invent a variation of the word—*aweful* (meaning full of awe and wonder).

To speak of *aweful* grace is to portray the feelings it evokes: awe, reverence, majesty, sublimity, wonder, and fear. But again, the word *fear* in this case may muddle clarity. Most people correctly use the term *fear* to denote anxiety caused by some impending danger or evil. Yet fear can also mean "to feel reverence for, to have a reverent awe of, to venerate . . ." Numerous biblical passages allude to this kind of awe-inspired "fear" with reference to God and creation, including the parallelism in the Thirty-third Psalm quoted above: "Let all the earth *fear* the Lord, let all the inhabitants of the world stand in *awe* of him!'' (verse 8, emphasis mine). Or in the book of Revelation an angel announces, ''Fear God and give him glory, for the hour of judgment has come; worship him who made heaven and earth, the sea and the fountains of water'' (14:7). Clearly, *fear* and *awe* here are terms of reverence and respect blended with a pinch of trepidation.

Anxiety (fear) and ugliness (awfulness) are readily distinguished from reverence and veneration (being awe-filled) in most biblical poetry and narrative. But our own feelings of awe and majesty are not as easily described when it comes to God and grace. We cannot summon emotions of sublimity on command as the Psalms seem to encourage. You can seldom successfully command yourself, ''Come now, it is time to feel a sense of awe.''

Rather, being *awed* is an unanticipated gift, an emotion that randomly strikes the heart—becoming awe-struck. Like the other elements of grace we have discovered, being awe-filled cannot be planned or earned. But it can grow out of the receptive attitude we cultivate. John R. W. Stott once was asked to describe his mental image of what it means to be a Christian. He replied that he imagined a person kneeling at an altar with other believers, head bowed, hands cupped together and lifted high waiting for the gift of communion bread to be placed in his hands. This reverent person faithfully awaiting the Eucharist in company with others is in many ways an excellent image. It is a picture of one who both anticipates and seeks, yet is one who humbly realizes communion with God is not a possession to grab but a gracious gift to be received with reverence, love, awe. It is a receptive posture, located in one of the places within God's creation where ''aweful'' grace is commonly found, in the context of the church and its worship and sacraments (as we will see).

To practice this figurative posture is a key element in preparing for grace. With hands held high in expectancy, we are better prepared to accept gracious gifts in humility. And with eyes and ears wide open, many forms of "aweful" grace are revealed in the vibrant world around us. The German language has a marvelous word for this cultivated attitude: *Weltwunder* (pronounced *veltvoonder*), being in "wonder of the world."

Honesty demands, however, that we cannot dwell exclusively upon those aspects of creation and beauty that inspire and nurture us. Nature can provide awful tragedies and aweful wonder alike. Natural disasters such as tornados, hurricanes, torrential floods, avalanches, and earthquakes all demonstrate that creation, too, has its dark side. Admittedly, some disasters are judgments humans pronounce upon themselves: dust bowl conditions created by improper soil conservation; polluted water and air produced by industrial carelessness or greed; the endangerment or extinction of rare animal species by reckless disregard for hunting laws; babies born deformed or handicapped due to drug-addicted parents; wars and the threat of nuclear cremation due to conflicting international interests.

But not all tragedies are the result of human error, of course. Creation's handiwork is also littered, as we well know, with mazing dangers and diseases, poisons and predators. Had I been more astute on the mountaintop at Hurricane Ridge, I would have better connected danger with the beauty. When I described the "snowcapped grandeur of Mounts Carrie and Olympus," I neglected to mention farther to the south and out of sight beyond the Olympic Peninsula stands Mount Saint Helens.

If this mountain is a "saint," it has a volcanically impious temperament. Long ago the Native Americans named it Lawala Clough, or Smoking Mountain. They believed (much like our thirty-eight-year resident of the Sheep Gate pool) that the adjacent Spirit Lake was inhabited by otherworldly spirits who seemed to disturb the water when it bubbled up under geothermal heat. You recall Mount Saint Helens unleashed a fitful eruption in May 1980, which spewed out a twelve-mile-high mushroom cloud of steam and dumped millions of tons of volcanic ash upon the northwestern United States and southwestern Canada. Nearly a hundred persons perished. A huge bomb-like crater now scars the mountain/volcano, a symbolic tribute to nature's explosive power.

Occasionally visible even farther south from Mount Saint Helens is Mount Hood in Oregon, where several inexperienced young mountain climbers on vacation were recently killed in a massive avalanche. These peaks were beyond my field of vision on the "mountaintop" at Hurricane Ridge. But the fact that they were out of sight did not lessen the devastation they had caused.

The harsh laws of nature do not yield to naiveté or innocence, to goodwill or mercy, to beauty or majesty. Every family knows that the bonds of love cannot shield loved ones from disease, accidents, and death; every faithful follower knows God's grace does not necessarily ensure good luck. Ensnared in this "veil of tears," every person must in some way come to grips with the real dangers and calamities of living at the foot of potential volcanos. Again the German language has a word to describe this aching awareness, the very sound of which spells anguish: *Weltschmerz* (pronouced *veltschmertz*), meaning "world pain" or "world-weariness."

Yet issuing from the combination of this aching but wonderful awareness is a profound affirmation of faith: God's grace has not abandoned the creation, which mixes beauty with hardship and danger. God's creation mingles "fear and awe," *Weltwunder* and *Weltschmerz*, wonder and pain. "Aweful" grace comes in those weak-kneed moments when something unexpectedly wonderful emerges anyhow despite the grime and tragedy. These are the graceful moments when innocence somehow triumphs beyond tragedy, when life goes on against all odds, when growth is nurtured in spite of apathy and entropy. This is not to say every cosmic evil has some preordained divine purpose. Evil stands contrary to good and God. Rather, these are moments of wonder at the very grace that allows life and beauty and hope to exist at all; they are rock-bottom realizations that in pain and boredom, no less than in gladness and joy, in Frederick Buechner's poignant words, "Life itself is grace."

Grace, Tim, And The Cheshire Cat

I once was captured by this innocently "aweful" grace beyond tragedy in an encounter with a young man named Tim. It happened when I was feeling somewhat sorry for myself. Difficulties of one kind or another seemed to encompass my world. A dear friend in my parish had just died of leukemia and I had recently discovered one of our lovely young families (with two small children) would soon be shattered by divorce.

So it was not with the best of moods that I went to a youth group meeting one hot summer Sunday afternoon. We were having a picnic outing at the park along with the youth group from a nearby church. Our congregation's newsletter reported it was to be the usual "food, fellowship, and fun," including softball, volleyball, and hot dogs—the only kind of "dogma" most youth groups relish.

Soon after my arrival I noticed Tim talking to some friends. He was a member of the other youth group and I had never seen him before. He was a very good-looking kid, about sixteen years old—that age when every single hair must be in place, the first driver's license is the passport to exotic new lands, jeans must have a designer label on the hip pocket, the age when a lone pimple on the nose seems as though it sticks out like the Matterhorn. While Tim was extremely handsome and had envious muscular development of his upper body, he had no legs. They had been amputated only inches below his torso, leaving only short stumps. He wore blue jean shorts rolled up tightly against what was left of his legs and fastened with safety pins. His wheelchair was completely pasted with all kinds of race car decals. The incongruity of racing cars on a wheelchair seemed a mocking monument to mobility.

My eyes were drawn to this extraordinary young lad as he grinned broadly and joked with his pals. It amazed me that there was not a trace of bitterness about him. He threw his head back and laughed as one prankster poured ice water down an adult counselor's back. He wheeled himself from group to group, mingling with everyone and introducing himself to those he did not know (including me). As I met him, suddenly my feelings of self-pity vanished. But this was not the "aweful" moment of grace.

I winced with pain for Tim when it was announced

the two youth groups would play each other in volleyball. How insensitive! I thought to myself. He seemed to be having such a grand time. "Won't volleyball exclude Tim?" I protested to the minister from the other church. The pastor only smiled back at me like a Cheshire cat as he strolled away nonchalantly in the direction of the volleyball court. I was *furious* at him!

The grass court was some yards away from our shelter house and the kids all walked to it as Tim struggled to roll his wheelchair over the rough sod. Now I was really fuming! Then I heard Tim taunt one of the kids in our group as he propelled himself, "You dudes don't have a chance against us. We're gonna *cream* you geeks." Of course, bold challenges among teenagers are never left uncontested, so all the way to the volleyball court Tim boasted and bantered with the others.

Finally we reached the court and each group took its place on opposing sides of the net. Tim navigated his chair directly beside one of the poles supporting the net and sat alone, suddenly silent, looking down and adjusting the pins on his pants. As I looked at him I felt awful. I assumed that he was sitting there on the sidelines too embarrassed to look up or speak, fidgeting with his safety pins to avoid making eye contact with all of us who were rudely excluding him from our game.

Just as the first serve was about to begin the contest, the unexpected moment of grace struck. Swiftly, Tim hopped down out of his wheelchair onto the ground. Using his knuckles as feet, his sturdy arms in tandem like one leg, and his stumps as the other leg, Tim rapidly scampered out (moving somewhat like a chimpanzee) and took his place on the court. Standing erect on what remained of his legs he was no more than three feet tall.

My pity turned to astonishment! I looked around with drooping jaw and discovered all the other kids were paying him no special attention. The Cheshire cat minister grinned at me from beyond the net.

In sheer awe I watched Tim position and balance himself on his stumps to return any ball hit in his vicinity. He exhibited amazing quickness and agility as he chased errant misses or dived and rolled after difficult shots. He proved to be a much better volleyball player than most of the other kids! His specialty was the "setting" position, whereby a player in the front row lofts the ball high while a teammate jumps to "spike" the ball over the net. My ever-smiling ministerial counterpart took particular delight when Tim set him up for a spike that he rocketed directly at me!

The whizzing ball knocked me down. The pastor/spiker leaned toward me and said through the net, "Just so you wouldn't feel excluded . . ." He was smirking, naturally.

By now I had to laugh at myself, too. I was slow getting up, and from my position on the ground I suddenly found myself at a curious angle, now looking *up* at Tim. He looked down on me, smiled, extended his hand, and asked, "Do you need some help getting up?"

Have you ever heard a Cheshire cat roar with laughter?

After the game we returned over the rough sod to the shelter house to eat hot dogs. This time Tim "walked" back in his unique fashion as the other kids took turns playfully rolling themselves (and pushing each other) in his wheelchair. I then noticed something special about the teenagers huddled around Tim that was different from others of that age group I've worked with over the years—these kids weren't playing the typical "put-down'' games. Nor were there the usual cliques dividing "popular" from "unpopular" kids. Most of them seemed to enjoy simply being themselves and generally accepting one another pretty well—qualities rare among teenagers! And all this genuineness appeared to revolve around Tim.

Several things about this encounter with Tim astounded me. The instant he tumbled out of his chair it seemed as if I were an eyewitness to Jesus' command, "Rise, pick up your pallet, and walk." No miracle happened in the sense that the inflexible laws of nature were repealed. But in the words of Gerald May, "Miracles are nothing other than God's ordinary truth seen with surprised eyes." And God's ordinary truth was that this young man displayed the miraculous resiliency of a grace-infused human spirit. Admiration and admonishment were mingled together as I humbly observed the graceful game from the sidelines. Tim was not handicapped by *my* narrow perception of what excluded him from being "normal." As I looked at how "normal" the other kids thought it was for Tim to scurry about, I was overcome with shame over having prejudged his abilities. I also painfully realized that most of my own pitiful complaints and imagined constraints were largely self-imposed. Tim helped remind me that many (though not all) boundaries of ability and achievement have more to do with laziness or stubborn refusal than actual limits. His acceptance of, yet transcendence beyond even very concrete limitations, inspired others around him to do likewise.

We cannot help but stand in awe of one who stands so gracefully on amputated legs. I later came to learn a bit more about the faith that undergirds Tim's "aweful" story. He was an orphan who had been adopted by one of those extraordinary families who accept only children with special problems. Tim's brothers and sisters included others who suffer from epilepsy, birth defects, severe emotional disturbances. Supporting this whole family are two parents who view these children as their distinctive "ministry." They are extremely humble people and don't feel they possess the gifts necessary for "public" ministry. Rather, they see themselves as trustees of God's special creation, stewards of these unique children who, for whatever dark quirks of nature or human nature, are sometimes hampered from a "normal" life. They count on the support of their church, and ofttimes crises or scheduling problems demand that they seek their congregation's help in caring for their family. Even with help from others, they love and care in circumstances that are certainly never easy. And not all their special children enjoy the mobility or the victories Tim does. But flowing from the grace that inspires their love is a stream of everyday miracles that reconnects a link of creation and redemption scarred by wounds that can never fully be understood or substantiated.

Surgeon, writer, and Yale professor of surgery Robert Selzer was witness to another graceful moment. In his book, *Mortal Lessons*, Dr. Selzer tells of an encounter after a tragically successful surgery he had performed:

I stand by the bed where a young woman lies, her face post-operative, her mouth twisted in palsy, clownish. A tiny twig of the facial nerve, the one to the muscles of her mouth, has been severed. She will be thus from now on. The surgeon had followed with religious fervor the curve of her flesh; I promise you that. Nevertheless, to remove the tumor in her cheek, I had to cut the little nerve.

Her young husband is in the room. He stands on the opposite side of the bed, and together they seem to dwell in the evening lamplight, isolated from me, private. Who are they, I ask myself, he and this wry-mouth I have made, who gaze at and touch each other so generously, greedily? The young woman speaks.

"Will my mouth always be like this?" she asks.

"Yes," I say, "it will. It is because the nerve was cut."

She nods and is silent. But the young man smiles.

"I like it," he says. "It is kind of cute."

And all at once I *know* who he is. I understand, and I lower my gaze. One is not bold in an encounter with a god. Unmindful, he bends to kiss her crooked mouth, and I am so close I can see how he twists his own lips to accommodate to hers, to show that their kiss still works. I remember that the gods appeared in ancient Greece as mortals, and I hold my breath and let the wonder in.[3]

In a world scarred by tragedies, we are still kissed by God's grace. To observe Tim chasing after stray volleyballs, to admire the incredible faith and patience of his remarkable family, to watch love accommodate itself to assure the beloved that devotion remains no matter what—all these demonstrate what it means to be kissed by grace. It is the grace that knows, yet transcends tragedy. To partake of and participate in this grace is, in fact, a kind of worship. To be sure, it is a different sort of inspiration than a mountaintop sunset or a stirring

sermon. Nevertheless, it is a worshipful, *aweful grace*
in that despite the very real tragedy of a young man who
will never know the full use of his legs or a young woman
with a severed facial nerve, the courage and steadfast
love that inspires people like that in turn inspires reverence, admiration, humble admonition, and respect. And
the source of this grace is mysteriously both beyond and
fully immersed in this ambiguity. From the personal experience of looking up to Tim I can assure you, after this
grace bowls you over and whizzes past you, you see it
most clearly from a ground-level posture, down on the
knees in stunned readiness.

Sacraments Of Grace

Worship, as Temple University professor Gerard
Sloyan once put it, "is to be in the presence of God in
a posture of awe." In this receptive posture, figuratively
or actually kneeling at the altar with hands lifted high,
we seem best able to receive this sacramental sort of
Presence. From within the context of the church and its
fellowship, the gathering of people who share life, beliefs, disbeliefs, faith, prayer, and worship, we sometimes glimpse gifts of grace better than when left to our
own devices. Meister Eckhart wrote long ago, "As thou
art in church or cell, that same frame of mind carry out
into the world, into its turmoil and its fitfulness."

David H. C. Read, native Scot and longtime pastor at
Madison Avenue Presbyterian Church in New York, tells
of a jolting experience that taught him a lesson about
worship and grace found amidst the "turmoil and fitfulness" of the world. In the winter of 1939, Read was in
Paris enjoying delightful meals and the comfortable com-

panionship of friends as he performed with relative ease his pastoral duties as chaplain to British troops stationed in France. Only days later, he found himself on a three weeks' march to a transit camp in Germany (as a prisoner of war, which he remained for the next five years!). In a mere three weeks, he confesses, his entire standards of value radically shifted.

Read recalls one day he was walking near the camp wire with two friends. In France, succulent dishes shared with friends were common fare. In the prison camp "all thoughts of rich meals vanished; our one thought was *bread*." There wasn't even enough bread to share communion together. As the friends were walking, they happened to pass under a machine-gun emplacement above the wire as a sentry was completing his breakfast. The guard thoughtlessly tossed away the crust of his bread. Read says, "Quick as lightning I flung myself on that crust, and we sat down on a stone and proceeded to divide that crust with the most meticulous accuracy into three equal pieces. For us it was manna from heaven as we ate and were thankful."[4]

Sometimes we must be jolted by such disparity into thanksgiving. We take for granted so easily the simple, sacramental elements of life symbolized by bread and wine. Yet these plain sacramental elements are often the very spiritual food that nourishes our growth in grace. These elements of grace are ones that have been faithfully passed on to us by generations of believers, persons who just like us faced an uncertain future, yet gathered anyhow to celebrate God's Presence through worship and the sacraments.

This passing of the sacraments of grace from generation to generation has silently occurred everywhere people gather to celebrate communion and baptism. A typical example is Mt. Zion United Methodist Church, a church near my home. Several generations have quietly come and gone since this little country church was erected over a hundred years ago. Its members have seen their share of tragedies and triumphs. Still, they gather every Sunday for worship and sacraments, just like scores of thousands of churches everywhere.

One Sunday morning, around the turn of the century, a volunteer was asked to provide the communion elements for the next worship service at Mt. Zion. Mrs. Clara Jackson had an arbor in her yard laced with grapevines, so she decided to help out. The next Sunday's communion service was graced by Clara's homemade grape juice and a special bread baked exclusively for communion at this tiny church. That morning a tradition was born at Mt. Zion. Each time the church shared communion, they prayerfully shared the fruit of Mrs. Jackson's love, grapes and bread symbolizing not only the body and blood of Christ, but also making real the union of creation and redemption, linking the ministry of the church and the labor of one's hands with the bounty of the earth.

After several decades Mrs. Jackson grew too old and feeble to continue her special ministry. Her daughter, Edith Street, decided she should take up the task, using the same grapevines and baking that same special bread in her mother's kitchen. All through the 1920s, the Depression years, World War II, the Cold War, Mrs. Street faithfully supplied the communion elements just as her mother had for twenty-five years before. No matter what happened in the tumultuous world outside the walls of Mt. Zion Church, they continued to gather, worship, break bread.

In time, Mrs. Street grew unable to continue. Sometime in the mid-1950s, Lela Steely, a lifelong friend of Mrs. Street, was given the two-generations-old recipes for the juice and bread. For nearly thirty years Lela continued the tradition, until her death in 1983. Since then, Mrs. Steely's daughter, Marie Byers, has taken up the duty along with her daughter, Barbara Baugh.

Mrs. Byers recalls one particular service that made her ponder all those who had preceded her. One autumn the congregation gathered in the church basement for an agape meal, to offer thanks for the completed harvest. Marie watched as her fellow parishioners shared the bread and juice she and her daughter had made. It was a special time as she thought about her mother, Mrs. Street, and Mrs. Jackson—Marie could even faintly remember when she was a small child visiting Mrs. Jackson nearly sixty-five years earlier. She thought about how the church had weathered much hardship. But they had stayed together and remained faithful, and had managed to pass down their traditions and wisdom. And behind it all, she somehow mysteriously felt herself part of this tradition of grace. In a quiet moment of *awe* she felt at one with God, her fellow church family, and the women who handed this great tradition down to her.

To partake of sacramental grace is to become mysteriously one with all the generations who have since paused to remember and commune with the One who said, "Take, eat, this is my body given for you." God's grace and Presence flow through the worship and the sacraments of the church, forming a long chain of tradition that links God's creation with redemption through

Christ and the church through the ages—the ''commun-ion of saints.'' It is an awesome and complex history, this story of communion, grace, and the church. Once again the Germans have a marvelous name for this—*Heilsgeschichte*, the ''history of salvation.''

An incident in my own life startled me with God's aweful, sacramental grace. It was a realization about my own baptism and its connections with the ''communion of saints,'' my own *Heilsgeschichte*.

In 1957 I was baptized in a small Methodist church in Indiana by Rev. Denzel Robertson. While I was only months old, he was nearing retirement. I never met him and he is now dead. But Rev. Robertson, or ''Pop'' as he was known, was by all accounts a vivacious old char-acter who had never married, dedicating himself solely to his church work. Rev. Robertson acquired the name Pop because he opened his home to many orphaned or troubled young men through the years, helping his ''sons'' get a new start in life.

My first childhood years were spent in the small com-munity of Milroy, Indiana. The Methodist church in town was an integral part of my extended family's life. My Methodist minister great-grandfather had retired there and my grandfather was the choir director at the church for several decades. Both my parents, several aunts and uncles, all sang in that choir while my sisters and I at-tended Sunday school with cousins and friends. Rev. Robertson, in true Methodist circuit-rider fashion, had moved to another church long before I was old enough to remember him.

Years later, while in college, I decided to pursue the path toward ordained ministry. Almost immediately I was made pastor of three small churches, one of which was the United Methodist Church in Waverly, Indiana.

After I had been pastor of this congregation for about a year, I happened to overhear one of the oldest church members say something about Denzel Robertson. The name dislodged a dim memory of the signature on my baptism papers. Offhandedly thinking it would be a quaint coincidence if the man who baptized me had at one time been pastor of this my first church, I asked her if indeed this Robertson had been a pastor. "Why yes, honey," she said. "Did you know him?"

"No," I answered. "When was he pastor here?"

"Pastor, here?" She chuckled. "Why honey, Denzel Robertson was never pastor here; he *grew up* in this church. He and I were baptized right here at this church on the same day!" She pointed precisely to the spot at the altar where the same oak baptismal font still stands. It probably hasn't been moved in a hundred years!

I told her Rev. Robertson had baptized me about twenty years before in Milroy. "That's nice, honey," she said, unmoved.

At the time I was not terribly moved, either, by this curious acquaintance with Rev. Robertson. But on the next Sunday, when I was the minister officiating at the baptism of a baby at the Waverly church, something happened that is awkward to relate. As I was holding that little bundle in my arms, preparing to baptize her, something suddenly came over me—there I was cuddling a baby in this church, myself a child baptized by a minister who in turn had received this sacrament in this very spot over eighty years earlier! I was standing at a five-generation crossroad of tradition. A whole web of relationships had come full circle. I began wondering: Could it be that the pastor of this church eighty years ago would have in his wildest dreams imagined such a scenario on the day he baptized the Robertson child? Might old Pop Robertson have had the foggiest notion when he baptized me that the squirming little Wimmer baby would someday walk in his life's shadow?

There was something sacramental about it all. It occurred to me that even when I was a helpless baby, there were family and ministers and Sunday school teachers and church members who pledged to nurture my spiritual growth, just as we do when any person is baptized into the faith. Reverend Robertson, and those who had baptized and nurtured him in this very church almost a century before, were somehow bound up together with God's timeless grace, the church, my parents' love, and my own infantile helplessness. Now I, too, was a "steward of the mysteries" of this grace. Who knows what network of spiritual influence this adorable little girl in my arms will grow to have? I wondered.

Swiftly, unexpectedly, in one wink of an eye, the weight of all this forced me to realize something in a completely new perspective. My life had been graced in ways I was only by accident coming to understand. How many more ways could I stand in awe of God's grace if I only knew other such undiscovered pieces of the puzzle? Who knows how much more influence my own little slivers of the "communion of saints" have had? Even the elderly woman who told me about Rev. Robertson was named *Grace*!

John Wesley, the founder of Methodism whom we met earlier, often spoke of "prevenient grace." The term *prevenient* comes from the old English usage of "prevent," which means "to go before" rather than to stop. Preventing or prevenient grace was for Wesley that aspect of God's grace that touches one even before one becomes aware of it. It is not a human ability to perceive one's sins or limitations. Prevenient grace is a gift from God that helps us to understand both our weaknesses and our dependency upon God's grace. Prevenient grace *prepares* us to comprehend both the need for grace and God's gracious offer of salvation. Most importantly for Wesley, prevenient grace is given to everyone so that each person may become more fully aware of God's grace in their lives.

Infant baptism—despite the doctrinal objections to it by some denominational traditions—is, in the Methodist tradition, a meaningful symbol of "prevenient grace" and of our helplessness before God. And in one fleeting moment, while standing at the altar of Waverly United Methodist Church coddling the newest in the long line of wriggling little Methodist babies, I came to understand for the first time how prevenient grace had been operative in my own life. God had been nurturing my growth and faith even when I was only a helpless baby. I was so overcome by the realization, I could not pronounce the words of baptism right away.

In that "aweful" moment—with misty eyes and my heart in my throat—the utter sacredness of it all fell on me like a torrent. A torrent of grace.

And so we have come full circle in our discussion of God's grace. We end as we began—by recalling the blessing given at the consecration of the Coventry Cathedral: "May God in the plentitude of his love, pour upon you the torrents of his grace." With this blessing have also come many challenges: to learn to rebuild our lives on a foundation of grace, even in the times when destruction and difficulty tend to make God seem distant.

The architect of the new Coventry Cathedral, Basil Spence, tells the story of how he once decided to rebuild his life. On June 8, 1944, two days after the invasion of Normandy, Spence tells how he saw something as a soldier he would never forget. At Oustreham and Hermanville, in Normandy, were two beautiful ancient Norman churches. They had stood for generations to represent the transcending presence of God. During the invasion, the Germans had placed two snipers in each church tower. In order to secure the area, two British tanks were brought up and in moments they had blasted away the belfry of each church. As a soldier, Spence was sorry there was no other way to remove the snipers—and as an architect, he felt as though he had witnessed the murder of a beautiful building.

Later that same day, Spence was dug in for the night just off the beaches of Normandy. An army friend, making conversation to ward off fear, asked Spence what was his chief ambition in life. The destruction of the churches he had seen that day prompted him to respond, "To build a cathedral."[5]

From destruction the idea of the Coventry Cathedral was born, though Spence did not yet know it. And just as the ruins of old St. Michael's Cathedral stand beside the new church as symbols of destruction and renewal, crucifixion and resurrection, the Coventry story and blessing stand as living reminders that your life, too, may be rebuilt on a foundation of grace—grace that is surprising, comforting, afflictive, costly, and aweful.

For these forms of grace—and many more—surround you constantly. And with eyes of faith to see, and ears of grace to hear, you may discern God's loving care that is with you always. All the moments of your life are moments of grace.

"Listen to your life," Frederick Buechner advises us, for "life itself is grace."

NOTES

Preface

1. *Martin Luther: Selections from His Writings*, John
   Dillenberger, ed. (Garden City: Doubleday,
   1961), p. 255. Emphasis added.
2. Leonardo Boff, *Liberating Grace* (Maryknoll, New
   York, 1979), p. 5.
3. Steve Harper, *John Wesley's Message for Today* (Grand
   Rapids: Zondervan, 1983), p. 40.

Chapter One

1. *The Oxford Book of Prayer*, George Appleton, ed. (New
   York: Oxford University Press, 1985), p. 172.

Chapter Two

1. Paul Tillich, "You Are Accepted," in *The Shaking of the
   Foundations* (New York: Scribner's, 1948),
   p. 161.
2. Robert McAfee Brown, *Creative Dislocation—Moments
   of Grace* (Nashville: Abingdon, 1980), p. 79.
3. Warren I. Susman, *Culture as History: The Transformation of American Society in the Twentieth Century*
   (New York: Pantheon, 1984). Also see David M.
   Potter, *People of Plenty: Economic Abundance and
   the American Character* (Chicago: University of
   Chicago Press, 1954).

4. Joseph A. Sittler, *Gravity and Grace* (Minneapolis: Augsburg, 1986), p. 31.

5. Paul Tournier, *Guilt and Grace* (San Francisco: Harper and Row, 1962), pp. 174ff.

6. Max Weber, *The Protestant Ethic and the Spirit of Capitalism* (New York: Scribner's, 1958).

7. St. Augustine, *Confessions*, in *The Living Testament: Essential Writings of Christianity Since the Bible*, M. Basil Pennington, Alan Jones, and Mark Booth, eds. (San Francisco: Harper and Row, 1985), p. 83.

8. Tillich, "You Are Accepted," p. 156.

9. C. S. Lewis, *Surprised by Joy: The Shape of My Early Life* (New York: Harcourt, Brace, 1955), p. 224.

10. Tillich, "You Are Accepted," pp. 161–62.

11. Doris Donnelly, "Is Spiritual Life for Everyone?" *Weavings* I (Sept/Oct, 1986), pp. 6–7.

Chapter Three

This chapter, and much of its language of the "maze," is conceptually indebted to Mark C. Taylor, *Erring: A Postmodern A/Theology* (Chicago: University of Chicago Press, 1984), especially chapter 7, "Mazing Grace."

1. Larry E. Axel, "Reshaping the Task of Theology," in Larry E. Axel and William Dean, eds. *The Size of God: The Theology of Bernard Loomer in Context* (Macon, Georgia: Mercer University Press, 1987), p. 61.

2. Ernest Hemingway, *A Farewell to Arms* (New York: Scribner's, 1929), pp. 327–8.

3. Cited in George A. Lindbeck, *The Nature of Doctrine* (Philadelphia: Westminster, 1984), p. 8.

4. Frederick Buechner, *Peculiar Treasures* (San Francisco: Harper and Row, 1979), p. 58.

5. Thomas P. McDonnell, ed. *A Thomas Merton Reader* (Garden Grove: Image, 1974), p. 16.

6. Thomas Merton, *The Sign of Jonas* (New York: Harcourt, 1953), p. 11.

7. Parker Palmer, *The Promise of Paradox* (Notre Dame: Ave Maria, 1980), p. 16.

8. Elie Wiesel, *Night* (New York: Avon, 1969), pp. 75–76.

9. Thomas Merton, *New Seeds of Contemplation* (New York: New Directions, 1961), p. 49.

10. Lewis B. Smedes, *Forgive and Forget: Healing the Hurts We Don't Deserve* (New York: Pocket Books, 1984), pp. 17ff.

11. John Patton, "Human Forgiveness as Problem and Discovery," *The Christian Century* (September 11–18, 1985), 102: 796, 797.

12. Elie Wiesel, *Somewhere a Master* (New York: Summit Books, 1981), pp. 11–12.

13. *Word and Witness*, October, 1984.

14. Reinhold Niebuhr, *The Irony of American History* (New York: Scribner's, 1952), p. 63.

Chapter Four

1. Miguel de Unamuno, *The Tragic Sense of Life*, Trans. J. E. Crawford Flitch (London: Macmillan, 1921), p. 330.

2. James L. Mays, *Amos* (Philadelphia: Westminster Press, 1969), p. 2

3. For an excellent book on biblical prophecy, see Joel Green, *How to Read Prophecy* (Downers Grove: InterVarsity Press, 1983).

4. Reinhold Niebuhr, *The Irony of American History* (New York: Scribner's, 1952), p. 38–39.

5. ibid., p. 169.

6. Carlo Carretto, *The God Who Comes*, cited in *A Guide to Prayer for Ministers and Other Servants*, Rueben P. Job and Norman Shawchuck, eds. (Nashville: The Upper Room, 1983), pp. 78–9.

7. Leonardo Boff, *Liberating Grace* (New York: Orbis, 1984), p. 85.

8. ibid., p. 154.

Chapter Five

1. Dietrich Bonhoeffer, *The Cost of Discipleship* (New York: Macmillan, 1963), p. 60.
2. *The Cost of Discipleship*, pp. 47–48.
3. ibid., pp. 59–60.
4. ibid., p. 99.
5. Mary Bosanquet, *The Life and Death of Dietrich Bonhoeffer* (New York: Harper, 1968), p. 66.
6. *The Cost of Discipleship*, p. 53.
7. Albert C. Outler, ed. *John Wesley* (New York: Oxford, 1964), p. 66.
8. William Willimon, *What's Right With the Church* (San Francisco: Harper and Row, 1985), p. 86.
9. ibid., pp. 86–87.

Chapter Six

1. Frederick Buechner, *Now and Then* (San Francisco: Harper and Row, 1983), p. 87.
2. Gerald G. May, M.D., *Addiction and Grace* (San Francisco: Harper and Row, 1988), p. 154.
3. Robert Selzer, *Mortal Lessons: Notes on the Art of Surgery* (New York: Simon and Schuster, Touchstone Edition, 1987), pp. 45–46.
4. David H. C. Read, cited in *Images of Faith*, Wendell Mathews and Robert P. Wetzler, eds. (St. Louis: Concordia, 1963), pp. 210–11.
5. Basil Spence, *Phoenix at Coventry: The Building of a Cathedral* (New York: Harper and Row, 1962), p. 1.

ABOUT THE AUTHOR

John Wimmer is a United Methodist minister who has served churches in Indiana and North Carolina. He is currently completing a Ph.D. in the History of Christianity at the Univeristy of Chicago Divinity School and lives in Indianapolis with his wife Jan. John is also the author of *No Pain, No Gain: Hope For Those who Struggle*.